HOUSING THE POOR:
AN OVERVIEW

HOUSING THE POOR: AN OVERVIEW

MORTON J. SCHUSSHEIM

Novinka Books
New York

Senior Editors: Susan Boriotti and Donna Dennis
Coordinating Editor: Tatiana Shohov
Office Manager: Annette Hellinger
Graphics: Wanda Serrano
Editorial Production: Maya Colmbus, Vladimir Klestov,
    Matthew Kozlowski and Tom Moceri
Circulation: Ave Maria Gonzalez, Vera Popovich, Raymond Davis, Melissa Diaz,
    Magdalena Nuñez, Marlene Nuñez and Jeannie Pappas
Communications and Acquisitions: Serge P. Shohov
Marketing: Cathy DeGregory

Library of Congress Cataloging-in-Publication Data
Available Upon Request

ISBN: 1-59033-724-7.

Copyright © 2003 by Novinka Books, An Imprint of
    Nova Science Publishers, Inc.
    400 Oser Ave, Suite 1600
    Hauppauge, New York 11788-3619
    Tele. 631-231-7269   Fax 631-231-8175
    e-mail: Novascience@earthlink.net
    Web Site: http://www.novapublishers.com

All rights reserved. No part of this book may be reproduced, stored in a retrieval system or transmitted in any form or by any means: electronic, electrostatic, magnetic, tape, mechanical photocopying, recording or otherwise without permission from the publishers.

The publisher has taken reasonable care in the preparation of this book, but makes no expressed or implied warranty of any kind and assumes no responsibility for any errors or omissions. No liability is assumed for incidental or consequential damages in connection with or arising out of information contained in this book.

This publication is designed to provide accurate and authoritative information with regard to the subject matter covered herein. It is sold with the clear understanding that the publisher is not engaged in rendering legal or any other professional services. If legal or any other expert assistance is required, the services of a competent person should be sought. FROM A DECLARATION OF PARTICIPANTS JOINTLY ADOPTED BY A COMMITTEE OF THE AMERICAN BAR ASSOCIATION AND A COMMITTEE OF PUBLISHERS.

Printed in the United States of America

Contents

Preface		vii
Chapter 1	Introduction	1
Chapter 2	Housing the Poor: Federal Programs for Low-Income Families	3
Chapter 3	Housing Construction and Rehabilitation Programs for Low-income Households	13
Chapter 4	Using the Existing Inventory of Housing	37
Chapter 5	Housing for Special Populations	45
Chapter 6	Community Development Block Grants and Other Programs	59
Chapter 7	Conclusions	73
Index		77

PREFACE

This book presents an overview of housing problems currently facing low-income families and individuals and trends that may accentuate or mitigate these problems. For one thing, rising rents in private rental housing associated with a robust economy are resulting in a dwindling supply of decent and affordable housing available to low-income households.

The book describes and assesses results of the main federal housing assistance programs for low-income households and special populations including the elderly, the disabled, and the homeless. Attention is directed to the historical roots of programs like public housing, rent certificates and vouchers and how changing circumstances or perspectives led to modifications and the shift in emphasis from project-based subsidies to tenant-based assistance, and from assisting the most vulnerable to rewarding more self-sufficient families. The way each program works is explained, along with a detailing of incomes, household composition, and other characteristics of families receiving benefits. Some facts are adduced on how programs have performed relative to their objectives.

Chapter 1

INTRODUCTION

Low-income families with housing problems are found in every section of the United States. They are located in large cities like Los Angeles and New York, but also in small towns and rural areas, in *colonias* on the border with Mexico, and on American Indian tribal areas of Arizona, New Mexico, and elsewhere. Long-term demographic and economic trends point to an increase in the number of low-income people with housing difficulties. Recent changes in welfare programs could accentuate these problems.

Since the 1930s a number of federal programs have been enacted to meet housing needs of low-income families. Most are administered today by the Departments of Housing and Urban Development (HUD) and Agriculture (USDA). The only ones — *standing alone* — that can reach the poorest of the poor are HUD's public housing and Section 8 rental assistance programs. Programs such as Low-Income Housing Tax Credits and HOME grants must be pieced together with other subsidies to provide housing affordable by poverty-level families. Families requiring less deep subsidies get help through a number of assisted housing programs. All eligible applicants for Section 8 rent vouchers face long waiting periods in most cities – up to 10 years in Los Angeles and Newark.

Current policies emphasize moving people from welfare to work, creating mixed-income developments, helping renters become homeowners, and shifting responsibility for managing and monitoring federal housing resources to local housing authorities, state housing finance agencies, and nonprofit entities.

The Quality Housing and Work Responsibility Act of 1998 and recent appropriations acts embody these objectives. Public housing agencies have been authorized to establish their own preferences in admission of tenants and to disregard previous federal preferences for families with the most severe hardships. Another provision targets public housing apartments to those with incomes higher than incomes of most current residents. Proponents believe that including more working families will result in healthier public housing communities. On the other hand, three-fourths of all tenant-based vouchers are now directed to those with extremely low incomes, giving them a chance to move to better neighborhoods.

These changes are occurring after years of constraint on spending for low-income housing. Budget authority for housing was sufficient to renew existing contracts, but little more. However, the fiscal year 1999 appropriation resumed funding of additional Section 8 tenant-based vouchers, providing for 50,000 new households moving from welfare to work, and the year 2000 funding allows for another 60,000 households. HUD requests 120,000 incremental Section 8 vouchers in its FY2001 budget. But tenant-based vouchers are not the whole answer. A congressional conference report on appropriations states that a shortage throughout the country of affordable rental dwellings also requires construction of housing targeted to low-income families.

Chapter 2

HOUSING THE POOR: FEDERAL PROGRAMS FOR LOW-INCOME FAMILIES

HOUSING PROBLEMS, CURRENT AND EMERGING

The quality of the nation's housing supply has markedly improved over the past half century. Most families live in houses in good condition, with adequate space, and pay a reasonable amount for shelter — generally less than 30% of monthly income. Two in three households are homeowners, with a median home value of $98,800 in 1997. Amidst this well-fixed population, however, commonly out of sight of the middle class, are families who cannot afford decent and adequate housing, those at the lowest rungs of the income distribution.

In American cities and towns, an estimated 600,000 individuals are homeless on any one night and more than 2 million persons including many children experience a period of homelessness at least once in the course of the year. Among those with some form of permanent shelter, 5.4 million unassisted, very-low-income renter households (12.3 million people) have severe housing problems, typically a heavy rent payment that leaves less than half of remaining income for food, medicine, and other essentials. And some families in both urban and rural areas have inadequate heating, lack complete kitchen facilities, or are without some basic plumbing.[1]

---

[1] Data are for 1997, the latest available. Source: *American Housing Survey for the United States: 1997*, U.S. Census Bureau, Current Housing Reports, issued September 1999 (subsequently referred to as AHS: 1997). See, also, *Rental Housing Assistance – The Worsening Crisis*, U.S. Department of Housing and Urban Development, March 2000. Estimate of 600,000 homeless by *The Urban Institute*.

Low-income Households

"Low-income" households for purposes of federal housing assistance are those with incomes at or below 80% of median income in the area, adjusted for number of persons in the household. "Very-low-income" households refer to those with incomes 50% of area median income or less; "extremely low-income" households are those with incomes 30% of area median income or below. Actual incomes of those eligible for housing aid vary from area to area.

Poverty Thresholds

Poverty thresholds are determined each year by the Census Bureau for the country as a whole. For 1999, the *national* poverty threshold for a three-person family with one minor child was $13,410 and for a four-person family with two minor children $16,895. These poverty thresholds are about 30% to 35% of median area income for such households in a number of metropolitan areas. Thus, families in poverty roughly correspond with those classified as extremely low-income for purposes of federal housing assistance.

THE MAIN HOUSING PROBLEMS BESETTING SOME AMERICAN FAMILIES

A Heavy Housing Cost Burden

This is the most pervasive housing problem for very-low-income Americans. In 1997, 5.4 million unassisted renters were classified by HUD as "worst case" households in need of housing subsidy, an increase of 200,000 over 1995.[2] Almost all of these households had very low incomes (less than 50% of median area income) and very high housing-cost burdens (over 50% of income); a small proportion were less burdened but occupied dwellings with severe physical defects.

---

[2] HUD defines households with "worst case" needs as unassisted renters with incomes below 50 percent of the local median who pay half or more of their income for rent and utilities or live in severely substandard housing.

Homeowners with heavy housing cost burdens (50%-99% of income) numbered almost 3.6 million. Two-thirds of these owner households had incomes less than $20,000.

A high housing-to-income ratio can be viewed as an *income* problem, but in this chapter it is discussed as a *housing* problem because shelter cost for most low-income families is the largest of the necessities.[3]

Defective Housing

Overall, housing standards in the United States have markedly improved since 1960, when 16% of all occupied units and 23% of occupied rental units were structurally unsound or lacked standard plumbing facilities.[4] Still, in 1997 with a total of 34 million occupied rental units, 1.1 million dwellings (3.2%) had, by HUD determinations, "severe" physical problems and 3 million (8.8%) had "moderate" physical problems. Specific deficiencies included 1.8 million without complete kitchens, and 669,000 lacking some or all plumbing facilities or without exclusive use for the household. Other occupied rentals had physical defects like bad electrical wiring, broken-down heating equipment, water leaks, and other evidence of poor upkeep.

A smaller proportion of the 65.5 million owner-occupied houses had similar deficiencies, but the numbers were not insignificant: by HUD criteria, 725,000 had "severe" physical problems and another 2.2 million had "moderate" physical problems. About 1 million had "moderate" heating problems, 515,000 homes were without complete kitchens, and 500,000 lacked some or all plumbing facilities.

As the housing stock ages, it requires increased expenditures for upkeep, repair, and rehabilitation to forestall serious building deterioration. This is a particular challenge for central cities, where the median age of occupied structures is about 40 years, and for many close-in suburbs as well. A majority of occupied dwellings with physical problems are more than 40 years old.

---

[3] Data for housing cost burden, substandard housing, and crowding are from the *AHS: 1997*.

[4] *Housing for the Poor: A Factual Background*, unpublished analysis prepared in 1965 by U.S. Housing and Home Finance Agency, based on U.S. Census of Population, 1960. A housing unit was defined as substandard if it was dilapidated or lacked inside hot and cold piped water, private inside toilet, or private bath or shower.

Crowding

This is still a problem although less common than several generations ago as household size has declined and dwellings have become larger. In 1997, by the standard of more than 1 person per room, 1.9 million renter households were crowded, 5.6% of all renter households. Crowding remains a serious problem for certain types of families and groups, particularly worst-case renters with children and Hispanic renters. One in five (18,6%) Hispanic renter households was crowded in 1997. Almost half (46.6%) of Hispanic renters had more than 1.5 persons per bedroom compared with about one in five (18.6%) non-Hispanic renters.

Neighborhood Problems

These problems external to the dwelling itself are a growing concern, not only in central cities but in suburbs as well. In 1997, almost 12 million households said they were bothered by street noise or traffic; more than 10 million were bothered by neighborhood crime. Large numbers were also troubled by odors, litter, or housing deterioration nearby, and unsatisfactory neighborhood shopping. Central city people cited crime as a leading bothersome condition, for suburbanites, traffic and noise were particularly bothersome. Middle-class families leaving central cities most commonly mentioned poor quality of urban schools and relatively high crime rates.[5] These responses are, at best, only rough indicators of neighborhood difficulties. In the worst neighborhoods, bad physical conditions coincide with deep social problems of concentrated poverty, joblessness, crime, drug abuse, and teenage pregnancy.

Homelessness

Homelessness is the lot of perhaps 600,000 persons on any given night. In the course of a year, an estimated 2.3 million persons may experience a period of homelessness at least once. At the end of the 1990s, the problem appeared as intractable as ever, while community patience seemed to have worn thin. In 24 out of 50 cities surveyed, police had initiated street sweeps

---

[5] *State of the Cities 1998*, U.S. Department of Housing and Urban Development, p. vii.

in the past two years, according to a law center.[6] In New York City, the mayor announced that the police would force street people into shelters or jail if they refused. At the same time, the mayor planned to evict families with children from shelters if an able-bodied parent refused to seek work. Advocates for the homeless in New York City deplored the policy, noting an increase in the number of homeless on the streets in the past year and a half and a severe shortage of beds in shelters.[7] In rural places where there are sparse or no services for the homeless, their numbers are probably substantially underestimated.

Segregation

Ethnic and racial enclaves have a long history in the United States. There were Irish areas, Little Italys, Polish districts, Jewish quarters, and black ghettos. Involuntary segregation of European immigrants and their descendants has all but disappeared, although there are still ethnic concentrations in cities and suburbs. Within cities, low-income minority families remain heavily segregated. Some deconcentration of metropolitan black households occurred between 1970 and 1997 — more than one-third (34.6%) were living in suburbs in the latter year compared to one-fifth in the earlier.[8] However, Census data reveal that a majority of black movers into suburbs are renters rather than owners;[9] most apparently live in predominantly black sections. While some dispersion has occurred, segregation continues to characterize living arrangements for the black population in both cities and suburbs.

PROBLEMS SPECIFIC TO RURAL AREAS

As with urban households, the main housing problem is burdensome housing costs, but significant numbers continue to live in houses with

---

[6] The National Law Center on Homeless and Poverty, reported in *The New York Times,* December 5, 1999, p. WK5.

[7] *The New York Times,* November 20, 1999, pp. A1, A11; December 1, 1999, p. A25; and Editorial, December 2, p. A30, December 3, 1999, p. C23.

[8] See Reynolds Farley and William H. Frey, "Changes in the Segregation of Whites from Blacks during the 1980s: Small Steps toward a More Integrated Society," *American Sociological Review,* Vol. 59, No. 1, February 1994, pp. 23-45. The proportion of metropolitan black households living in suburbs was 34.6 percent in 1997 as derived from *AHS: 1997,* Table 5-1.

[9] *AHS: 1997,* Table 5-11.

physical deficiencies. In 1997, 1.8 million occupied dwellings in nonmetropolitan areas (both renter and owner-occupied) had moderate or severe physical defects such as inadequate heating or lacking some or all plumbing. The grim housing conditions of domestic farm workers, especially those who follow the crops, have been documented in congressional hearings and other surveys.[10] Native Americans in tribal areas occupy some of the worst houses in the country, many without basic plumbing.[11] These problems are discussed in more detail below.

TRENDS

Current housing problems are likely to be exacerbated by long-term trends in population change, rental housing markets, and shifts in social legislation.

- *Demographics.* Migration into the United States, particularly from Mexico and other Latin American countries but also from Asia, is projected to add substantial numbers to some cities and towns between 2000 and 2005. Like earlier immigrants, many of these newcomers are finding their way into the labor force, paying their way, and benefiting the economy.[12] Still, many need special services and larger housing units than are generally available to those with entry-level wages. Hispanic renters not only comprise about half of all crowded renter families in the country but typically pay more of income for rent.

- *Dwindling Stock of Affordable Private Rentals.* A steady decline since the 1970s in the supply of rental housing affordable by low-income renters continued unabated. Between 1996 and 1998, the number of privately-owned dwellings renting for less than $300 a

---

[10] See, for example, *Migrant and Seasonal Farmworker Housing in the United States,* Hearing before the Subcommittee on Housing and Community Development of the Committee on "Banking, Finance and Urban Affairs, House of Representatives," 97th Congress, September 1981-January 1982. The subcommittee Chairman, Henry B. Gonzalez, cited a study finding a need for 1.2 million housing units for migrant and seasonal farmworkers; only one-third that number of decent units were actually available at the time.

[11] *Taking Stock of Rural Poverty and Housing for the 1990s,* The Housing Assistance Council, Washington, DC, 1994, p. 55.

[12] National Academy of Sciences, *The New Americans,* National Research Council, Washington, DC, cited in The U.S. Department of Housing and Urban Development, *The State of the Cities, 1998,* p. 62.

month (adjusted for inflation) fell from 6.8 million to 5.5 million, a 19% decline. The ratio of affordable rental units available to extremely low-income renters (incomes of 30% or less than area median) declined from 48 per 100 to 36 per 100 between 1989 and 1997, and was probably lower in 2000.[13]

- *Losses in Assisted Housing Supply.* More than 1.6 million households live in HUD-aided units with assistance linked to specific projects. Some of this supply could be lost due to shoddy initial construction, deferral of repairs, or hard use. Other good-quality projects in desirable locations may be lost as contracts expire and owners opt to convert them to market-level rentals. "Enhanced vouchers" under Section 8 will enable most of these tenants to remain in their apartments, but over time as they leave the units will be lost to the assisted housing supply. Losses could also occur in rural-based rental projects of the Department of Agriculture, which now shelter about 450,000 families. Over half of these buildings are over 15 years old and could deteriorate without substantial rehabilitation or repairs.

- *Welfare Reform.* Changes in federal welfare legislation and state policies will also affect efforts to meet housing needs of low-income people. Between March 1994 and June 1999 the number of families receiving welfare assistance dropped by half-from 5.1 million to 2.5 million families (from 14.2 million persons to 6.9 million persons).[14] State agencies are supposed to keep track of families going off welfare, but little is yet known about their current housing circumstances.

Under welfare reform — the Personal Responsibility and Work Opportunity Reconciliation Act of 1996-able-bodied adults in welfare families are required to seek work. Those who fail to secure or hold jobs and lose some or all of their welfare checks will have difficulty paying their rent. Most welfare families do not receive housing assistance other than what is

---

[13] U.S. Department of Housing and Urban Development, *Waiting in Vain: An Update on AMERICA's Rental Housing Crisis,* March 1999, p. 13; *and Rental Housing Assistance – The Crisis Continues,* April 1998, p. 11.

[14] U.S. Department of Health and Human Service, *HHS News,* August 20, 1998; also, *Temporary Assistance for Needy Families (TANF): 1936-1996,* updated January 1998, Administration for Children and Families, U.S. Department of Health and Human Services, http://www.acf.dhhs.gov/news/3697.htm. Prior to 1996, the program was called Aid to Families with Dependent Children (AFDC).

included in their welfare check for shelter. Some may have to move in with relatives or friends; others could become homeless. The low-end, privately-owned rentals occupied by welfare families (without rental assistance under HUD programs like Section 8) are commonly under-maintained. If families lose their income supports, owners of such houses will have even less incentive or ability to maintain them, and some properties may well be abandoned.[15]

There could be consequences, also, for welfare families in HUD-assisted public and private developments. In 1999, 700,000-800,000 households receiving housing assistance under various HUD programs reported "welfare" as their main source of income (Temporary Assistance for Needy Families or General Assistance but not Supplemental Security Income or Social Security). Adult members, usually single mothers, are mandated to find jobs. A preliminary study by HUD notes that mandated residents are competing for entry-level jobs with non-welfare persons. They may live far from job centers. Success or failure will vary from one metropolitan area to another depending upon the demand for labor, the adequacy of transportation, or the possibility of moving closer to places of employment. Further, lack of job experience and under-education are major hurdles to successful transition from welfare to work.[16] However, a positive finding (not specific to HUD-assisted families) is that the rate of employment and incomes of families moving from welfare to work increased between 1996 and 1997.[17] From 1997 to 1998 the proportion of TANF adults employed rose from 13.3% to 22.8%. But average cash benefits plus average adult earnings were only slightly above $400 a month in 1998.[18] Monthly housing costs alone for most renter households in 1997 exceeded $400.

If many work-mandated public housing adults fail to get and keep full-time jobs, their rent-paying ability will drop and reduce rent receipts of the public housing agency (PHA). These agencies would have to seek additional operating subsidies from the federal government or from state and local governments, and/or raise minimum rents, or reduce the number of failed work-mandated families. The consequences will vary among PHAs around

---

[15] See *The State of the Nation's Housing: 1997*, op. cit., pp. 21-22.
[16] *Welfare Reform Impacts on the Public Housing Program: A Preliminary Forecast*, U.S. Department of Housing and Urban Development, 1998.
[17] *HHS News*, August 20, 1998, cited above. The First Annual Report to Congress on the Temporary Assistance to Needy Families program from the U.S. Department of Health and Human Services noted that 1.7 million adults on welfare in 1996 were working in 1997, a nearly 30 percent increase.
[18] Source: unpublished Congressional Research Service tabulations of the *FY1998 TANF Emergency Data Report* sample file.

the country depending upon the proportion of mandated residents needed to work to maintain current rent levels, the strength of local job markets, minimum rent policies, and other factors.

Figure 1. Federally-Assisted Rental Housing Units by Program: 1998

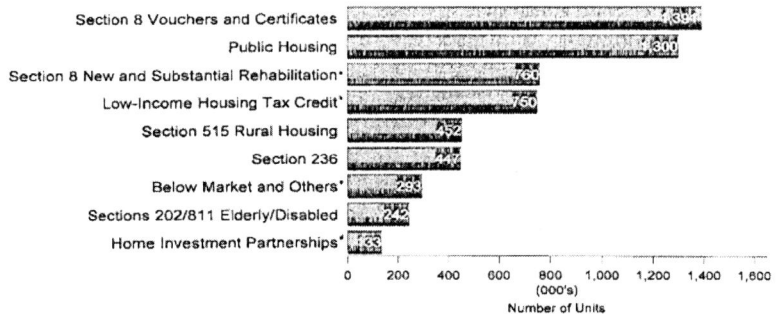

[a] Includes Section 8 Moderate Rehabilitation; does not include Sections 202/811 housing for the elderly and disabled.
[b] Substantial overlap with Section 8 and HOME.
[c] BMIR 221 (d)(3) plus rental assistance program, rent supplements, loan management set-aside, and property disposition.
[d] An additional 133,000 completed units are for homeowners and homebuyers.
Source: U.S. Department of Housing and Urban Development and U.S. Department of Agriculture.

CURRENT LOW-INCOME HOUSING PROGRAMS

A medley of federal programs address low-income housing problems. The Department of Housing and Urban Development is the lead agency in these efforts in which a number of departments are also involved, including the Department of Agriculture and the Treasury Department's Internal Revenue Service (IRS), the latter through tax incentives. In 1998, about 4.8 million households or units were receiving subsidy payments under HUD programs and up to one million low-income families were participating in assisted housing programs of the Department of Agriculture. A low-income housing tax credit authorized in 1986, overseen by IRS and administered by state and local housing finance agencies, has provided equity capital for the construction or rehabilitation of 700,000 to 800,000 units, most of which have also received Section 8 project-based or tenant-based assistance, HOME funds, or other types of subsidies. Block grant funds are being used by localities for a variety of purposes including rehabilitation and construction of housing affordable by low-income families. The levels of the various renter-assisted housing programs in 1998 are shown in Figure 1.

What follows is a discussion of some of the main low-income housing programs — how they work, whom they serve, and issues associated with their operations and continuation. The programs are grouped by goals or means of carrying out goals. Some programs have several goals, so groupings are somewhat arbitrary. For example, the HOME program facilitates the construction or rehabilitation of housing; it also contributes to community improvement. Here, it is listed with construction and rehabilitation approaches.

Chapter 3

HOUSING CONSTRUCTION AND REHABILITATION PROGRAMS FOR LOW-INCOME HOUSEHOLDS

PUBLIC HOUSING

This is the oldest federal low-income housing program, initiated in the 1930s as a public works effort to help boost a deeply depressed economy. Today, 3,400 public housing authorities, located in every region of the country, manage 13,900 projects containing 1,300,000 units and about 3 million persons. Most projects provide adequate housing, but some have serious problems — buildings in need of substantial rehabilitation or replacement, locations in neighborhoods with high concentrations of poor families, or high vacancy rates (10% overall in 1998). Tenants, lacking sufficient income to move to market-priced housing, have had little leverage over managers with regard to provision of services. These drawbacks are partially addressed by recent administrative policy changes and legislation, discussed below.[19] But for all its problems, public housing continues to attract low-income applicants: about 1 million families were on waiting lists of 40 local authorities in 1998, with an average wait of 33 months in the largest cities. In Los Angeles and Newark, the waiting period was up to 10 years.[20]

---

[19] A big drawback of public housing, as seen by some economists, is lack of choice for tenants. Once they get assistance, it comes in the form of an apartment-period. The same criticism is made of other project-based assisted housing programs for low-income persons.

[20] *Waiting in Vain,* cited above, pp. ii-iv, 7.

Established on a permanent basis by the United States Housing Act of 1937 (some projects had been constructed earlier by the Public Works Administration and the Farm Security Administration), public housing was intended to stimulate construction activity, clear slums, and provide low-rent housing. The framers thought that most tenants would be working class and would move on when their economic situation improved. This, indeed, happened with many residents in the early years of public housing.

How the Program Works

The housing is built and operated by local PHAs established under state enabling legislation. While nominally independent of local general governments in many jurisdictions, the PHA must get approval of proposed projects from the city council or county government.[21] The local government helps to reduce rents by allowing the PHA to pay a small percentage of rent receipts instead of property taxes that would be levied on private landlords. The main support for public housing, however, comes from the federal government: contracts or grants cover development and modernization costs; annual subsidies also cover the bulk of operating expenses, something not contemplated in the original legislation. Because of the deep subsidies, housing authorities have been closely regulated by the U.S. Department of Housing and Urban Development and its predecessor agencies. However, recent legislation allows PHAs more flexibility in making management decisions such as setting criteria for selecting tenants.

Who are Served

The 1.2 million households now living in public housing are among the poorest families in the nation. Resident households have an average income of $9,100. Those mainly dependent upon welfare (TANF, short for Temporary Assistance for Needy Families formerly known as AFDC, or General Assistance from state or local governments) comprise 18%. Others report as the main income source Social Security, Supplemental Security Income, child support, unemployment benefits, pensions, or a mixture of

---

[21] Under state housing authorities law in 12 states, it is permissible (and in some cases mandatory) that public housing powers be exercised by city agencies rather than by separate public housing authorities. Such laws are found in California, Michigan, New York, and Oregon, among others. Source: Office of General Counsel, U.S. Department of Housing and Urban Development.

sources. However, one in four families (24%) derives most of its income from wages, business, or both. The average income of households in public housing and other rent-assisted housing programs is shown in Figure 2.

One-parent families with children occupy 39% of all accommodations and two-parent families with children 6%. Elderly households (62 or older), occupy about one-third of the units. A growing clientele are non-elderly persons with disabilities (head or spouse), who constitute 24% of all public housing households. Two-thirds of public housing families are minority, including 47% black and 19% Hispanic.[22] The composition of households in public housing and two other assisted housing programs is shown in Figure 3.

Figure 2. Average Income of Households in Selected Renter-Assisted Housing Programs: 1998

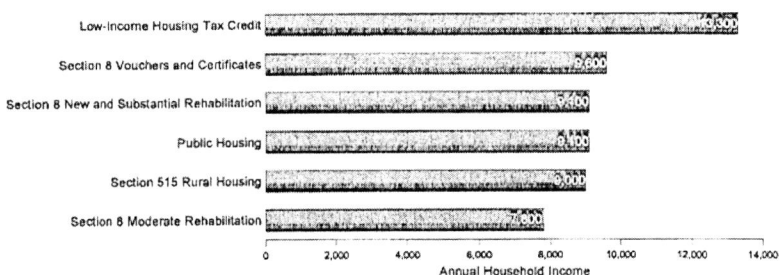

Note: Incomes shown are before adjustments, which may reduce the tenant's Income for rent-paying purposes by $400 or more. Incomes are for 1998 except Section 515 Rural Housing (1999) and Low-Income Tax Credit (1996).
Source: *A Picture of Subsidized Households in 1998,* U.S. Department of Housing and Urban Development; records of U.S. Department of Agriculture; U.S. General Accounting Office.

---

[22] *A Picture of Subsidized Households in the United States: United States Summaries,* by Paul Burke, U.S. Department of Housing and Urban Development, August 28, 1998.

Figure 3. Household Composition in Three Assisted-Housing Programs

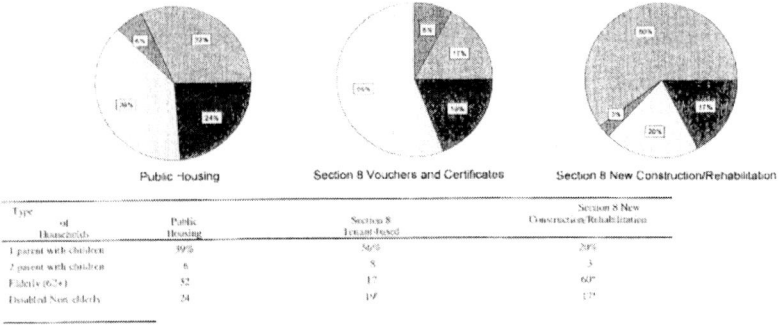

Type of Households	Public Housing	Section 8 Tenant-Based	Section 8 New Construction/Rehabilitation
1 parent with children	39%	54%	20%
2 parent with children	6	8	3
Elderly (62+)	32	17	60*
Disabled Non-elderly	24	19	12*

^a Includes Section 202 housing units for the elderly.
^b Adjusted for overlap with households with children.
Source: *A Picture of Subsidized Households in 1998,* U.S. Summaries, U.S. Department of Housing and Urban Development, August 28, 1998.

Locations

From the beginning, public housing was opposed in many neighborhoods. Some if not all developments had to be located near railroad tracks, highways, or industrial zones, and almost always — in North and South — in racially separated parts of town. The scarcity of suitable sites and rigid cost limitations resulted in medium to high density developments in large cities recognizable as "the projects." In hindsight, critics have asked how the local officials in charge could have picked such bad locations. In no small measure, the explanation is that private owners, neighborhood groups, and their aldermen did not want public housing nearby.[23] Almost half (46%) of public housing units are in large projects containing 200 or more units. Since 1970, however, almost all developments *for families* have been placed on sites with no more than 50 units. Developments for the elderly have encountered less neighborhood resistance, and tend to be better located and designed than family housing.

---

[23] Coleman Woodbury, an early public housing advocate and one-time vice chairman of Chicago's public housing authority, offered this explanation in an oral history conducted by the writer in November 1993. *Pioneers in Housing,* Library of Congress, unpublished.

Tenant Selection and Preferences

In the early years, applicants were carefully screened for good housekeeping, conventional family relationships, and working class background. Standards were relaxed, however, during the 1950s and 1960s as public housing agencies came under pressure to admit families displaced by urban renewal and highway construction and to take in single-parent families with very low incomes.

With far more applicants than openings, policy has oscillated between helping the neediest and having a wider mix of incomes. In general, occupancy has been limited to households with incomes up to 80% of area median income, with a portion designated for "very-low-income" households, those with incomes of 50% or less than area median, with adjustments for smaller and larger families. Within these income limits, households occupying substandard housing or involuntarily displaced received preference under legislative amendments in 1979; those spending half or more of income for rent were given preference by federal law in 1983. But local preferences were permitted and gradually expanded, to 30% of units available for occupancy in any year by 1990 legislation, and to 50% in 1992.

Since 1996, PHAs have been permitted to use local preferences for admission, first by language inserted into annual appropriation acts, now permanently by authorizing legislation enacted in 1998. To increase rent receipts and to limit the number of families that are most expensive to accommodate, local authorities are expected to select families with higher incomes than under earlier federal preferences.

Operating Subsidies

Under the original funding formula, federal payments covered only debt service on bonds issued to build public housing. Rents collected from tenants were to cover all operating expenses; but in time, this resulted in heavy rent payments for very low income families. In 1969, Congress amended the statute to limit rent to 25% of adjusted family income. This limitation threatened the financial solvency of some PHAs, and in 1970, legislators approved the payment of operating subsidies.[24] Subsidies to cover the

---

[24] The 1969 limitation on rent that could be charged tenants is known as the Brooke amendment. The 1970 authorization of operating subsidies was not the first; in 1961, such

growing gap between operating costs and rent receipts have mounted over the years. Currently, most tenants pay 30% of income in rent, but rent collections cover, on average, less than 40% of operating and maintenance expenses. In 1998, rent and utilities paid by tenants averaged $193 per month. The federal government's cost per unit for operating subsidies averaged $187 per month.[25] The operating subsidy a PHA receives each year is determined by a Performance Funding System formula established by HUD.

Modernization

Public housing is an aging stock, at least half built before 1970. As with older privately owned structures, major elements wear out and need replacement or repair, such as heating and electrical systems, roofs, kitchens and bathrooms. But public housing authorities have been unable to set aside funds from their own receipts to deal with major replacements and repairs on a regular schedule. Federal support has been provided but not in sufficient amount to prevent a huge backlog of modernization needs from accumulating in this $90 billion inventory. Government spending per unit for modernization averaged $162 a month in 1998.

A Public Housing Capital Fund was authorized in 1998 as part of major public housing reform legislation (discussed below). This fund consolidates previous programs including public housing modernization, public housing development, and major reconstruction of obsolete public housing programs. Funds may be used for technical assistance as well as hard costs. Also, the 2,400 smallest PHAs are now getting capital funds by formula rather than competition, giving them more flexibility and predictability in addressing modernization, deferred maintenance, and other responsibilities.

Drug Elimination

Low-income people are often victims of crime and drug operations wherever they live. Public housing residents are vulnerable because they are so concentrated. Although drug activity may be brought into the developments by non-residents, it then may involve residents drug use and

---

payments were approved in connection with units occupied by elderly households if required to maintain the solvency of a low-rent project.

[25] *A Picture of Subsidized Households,* cited above.

drug-associated crime rose alarmingly in the 1980s. Congress responded by authorizing a Public Housing Drug Elimination Program in 1988. HUD has made more than 4,000 grants totaling $1.3 billion in the period 1989-1997. Two thirds of the money has been used for law enforcement and crime prevention activities; other funded activities are resident patrols to report on crime, physical improvements in or around the projects, and treatment of drug abusers. Grants are awarded on a competitive basis to public and Indian housing agencies with the most severe problems and a long-term strategy to deal with them. But the annual competitive application procedure and associated uncertainty mean that PHAs cannot carry out continuous programs, according to public housing spokesmen.[26] The fiscal year 2000 appropriation provides $310 million for drug elimination, the same as for 1999. This includes $20 million for a New Approach Anti-Drug program to augment security and hold down drug-related criminal activity.

Management Difficulties

Effective management of public housing calls for the professional skills of private real estate managers and more. Public housing managers must see that heat is maintained and water leaks fixed but also must integrate social services, implement income checks and work requirements, deal with drug activity on the property, and provide security for the majority of law-abiding residents.

Most local authorities are performing up to standards set by HUD, but not all. Following instructions by Congress, HUD established a list of troubled housing agencies based upon indicators of poor management performance. Among the indicators are high vacancy rates, uncollected rents, poor maintenance, delayed work orders, inadequate security, shortfalls in resident services and community building, lags in modernization, failure to make systematic inspection of units and heating and other systems, and inept financial management. In December 1999, 44 PHAs were on HUD's troubled list, down from 53 in August 1998. Housing authorities on the troubled list are closely monitored and may be placed into receivership.

In fact, some formerly troubled PHAs are being managed by receivers with arguably good results. A notable example is the District of Columbia's agency. Over a four-year period, a court-appointed receiver effected a turn-

---

[26] Council of Large Public Housing Authorities (CLPHA), *Basic Facts About Public Housing*, Washington, DC, February 1993, pp. 8-9.

around that resulted in HUD removing the agency from the troubled list in April 1998.[27]

HUD is now starting to implement a more comprehensive evaluation process called the Public Housing Assessment System. Public housing agencies will be scored by physical condition, financial management, management operations, and resident participation. Performance of each local agency will be rated High, Standard, or Troubled. A PHA may be listed as Troubled by reason of physical condition, financial deficiencies, or other factors. Real scores are to be issued in June 2000 based on performance as of March 31. Advisory assessments indicate that as many as 500 local public housing agencies could be scored as Troubled under this new system.

The fairness and workability of the new system have been questioned by industry and congressional critics and is the subject of an examination by the General Accounting Office (GAO). Conferees on the HUD FY2000 appropriation directed HUD to consult with PHAs and review the GAO study before issuing a consensus-based final rule on the new assessment system. The conferees further instructed HUD to "acknowledge the complexities and practicalities inherent in managing large-scale apartment buildings and make allowances for these considerations."

HOPE VI-Revitalizing Severely Distressed Public Housing

A major overhaul of public housing is well underway. Under a program authorized in 1992 known as Hope VI, local agencies are trying to turn severely distressed projects into more livable communities by reducing densities and attracting families with incomes substantially higher than those of current residents. The idea is to create mixed-income communities with more working families and role models for less functional families. Some of the worst public housing developments are being demolished. A HUD goal is to approve "the demolition of 100,000 blighted or obsolete units by the year 2003, and [provide] essential replacement housing... ."[28] Replacements would be low-density developments into which some of the former residents could move. Other displaced families would be given vouchers to enable them to seek housing elsewhere. For revitalization of severely distressed

---

[27] However, the Washington, DC Housing Authority had a poor record in using Section 8 certificates in 1999. HUD recaptured a sizable amount of funds that the local agency failed to use. Source: Unpublished data from HUD budget office.

[28] *The FY1999 Budget of the U.S. Department of Housing and Urban Development, February 1998, p. 24.*

public housing under HOPE VI, the FY2000 appropriation provides $575 million, a reduction of $50 million from the President's request and the amount actually funded in FY1999.

1998 Legislation

The Quality Housing and Work Responsibility Act of 1998 (Public Law 105-276) is a sweeping restructuring of the public housing program.[29] It authorizes HUD to deregulate PHAs performing at an acceptable level and reduces reporting requirements. The law contemplates that more working and upwardly mobile families will be brought into public housing. It allows housing agencies to reserve up to 60% of units becoming available for families with incomes above 30% of area median income. Forty (40) percent of new admissions to public housing must be designated for families with incomes below 30% of area median, although the local agency may choose to admit a larger percentage.

As noted, the new law permanently rescinds federal occupancy preferences that targeted dwellings to some of the neediest families — those living in substandard housing (including the homeless), involuntarily displaced families, and those spending 50% or more of income on housing. PHAs are permitted to set preferences based on local housing needs and priorities. The intent is to deconcentrate poverty in certain projects or buildings and to promote income mixing by bringing higher income families into lower income projects, and the reverse. The deconcentration process must be detailed by the PHA in an annual plan submitted to HUD. The expectation is that over time the occupants of public housing will constitute a broader economic and social mix than the current occupancy.

There are provisions to encourage residents to increase their work effort. For one, increased income from employment of adult family members is disregarded for 12 months after the income improves. The rent increase after 12 months is phased in over a two-year period. In lieu of an income disregard, the resident may request that the PHA establish an individual savings account for that family. Moreover, a tenant may annually choose to pay a flat rent rather than a rent based on income. If the family's income subsequently falls due to loss of a job or other financial hardship, the housing agency must promptly permit the family to switch to an income-based rent.

---

[29] Enacted as Title V of H.R. 4194, Departments of Veterans Affairs and Housing and Urban Development, and Independent Agencies Appropriations Act, 1999.

Another new provision requires that able-bodied adults in public housing who are not employed or participating in a family self-sufficiency program contribute 8 hours each month to community service. Residents who fail to comply may have their lease terminated.

The 1998 legislation also enables PHAs to obtain police records to screen applicants and to evict residents who use drugs or abuse alcohol. Tenants could be evicted for criminal activities committed by a household member within or outside of public housing. A controversial provision in the law requires applicants to sign an authorization for the release of information by drug treatment centers about current use of illegal drugs.[30] The latter provision was opposed by health care providers on grounds that it violates the confidentiality of medical records.

Most advocacy groups generally welcome provisions to increase resident participation in decision-making through resident advisory boards and a requirement that at least one resident be a member of the PHA's governing board.[31] Some are critical of the mandatory contribution of community service by unemployed public housing residents. Others note that the reservation of available dwellings for the lowest income group (below 30% of area median income) could be satisfied in some metropolitan areas without reaching down to families living on a minimum wage or on welfare.[32]

There are numerous other provisions applicable to public housing in the 1998 Act, including: authority to PHAs to impose minimum rents to increase receipts; criteria for demolition or disposition of public housing projects; and conversion of public housing stock into vouchers for use elsewhere by residents in occupancy. The legislation also modifies the tenant-based and project-based Section 8 programs, as described below.

Appropriations

Large housing authorities for the most part support the new approaches since they will have more discretion in operating their projects. They note, however, that it will take time to see positive results from deregulation. They have been urging a substantial increase in funds for operating subsidies and

---

[30] See *CRS Report 98-443E, Housing Authorization Bills: Overview of H.R. 2 and S. 462*, May 8, 1998, by Susan Vanhorenbeck.
[31] *Critical Issues Pending in Public and Assisted Housing Reform Legislation: H.R. 2 and S. 462*, cited above.
[32] Deborah Austin and Nancy Bernstine, "Public Housing Unchained?" in *Shelterforce*, September/October 1997, #95.

modernization.[33] The FY2000 appropriation for operating subsidies is set at $3.138 billion, an increase of $320 million over 1999. The appropriation provides $2.869 billion for public housing capital improvements, a decrease of $100 million from 1999, but larger by $400 million than for 1998. As in 1999, the funds will be used in part to lower backlogs in necessary repairs, to build replacement units for demolished structures, and to continue assistance to displaced families.

Current Activities

Even before the 1998 legislation, reform had begun in some cities. Densities are being lowered by selective demolition of buildings and replacement by townhouses and other types of structures that do not appear or function like "the projects." Some of the new construction is being provided by nonprofit organizations utilizing other types of financing such as the low-income tax credit (described below). Demolition and conversions to mixed-income developments are taking place in the Anacostia section of the District of Columbia and in scores of neighborhoods around the country.

INTEREST REDUCTION PROGRAMS: SECTION 221(D)(3) BELOW MARKET INTEREST RATE (BMIR) PROGRAM AND SECTION 236

A housing program for low- and moderate-income families and displaced families was introduced in the Housing Act of 1961 (Public Law 87-70). The Federal Housing Administration was authorized to insure mortgages on rental housing developments at a below-market interest rate and low or no insurance premiums and other liberal provisions. The interest rate, based on the average market yield on all outstanding marketable obligations of the federal government, was initially a little over 3% and later set at a flat 3%.

---

[33] CLPHA News, March/April 1998, Washington, D.C.

How the Program Worked

Borrowers could be nonprofit entities, limited dividend companies, cooperatives, and certain public bodies other than public housing authorities. The Federal National Mortgage Association, then a government agency, was authorized to purchase the below-market interest mortgages under its special assistance program. This was known as "backdoor financing" and was disfavored by Treasury Department and Bureau of the Budget (BOB) officials. Housing policymakers reportedly designed this approach because they viewed it as more likely to win approval at the time than a direct loan proposal.

Who are Served

Intended beneficiaries were families with incomes too high for public housing but too low to afford decent dwellings in the private rental market. In 1998, household income in BMIR projects not receiving substantial additional subsidy averaged $22,000. Three-fourths (73%) of these residents reported wages as the major source of income and very few (3%) were dependent upon welfare. Rents paid by tenants averaged $362 a month.[34]

Households in BMIR projects receiving additional subsidies such as Section 8 "Loan Management Set Aside" had an average income of $12,000 with almost half (47%) reporting wages as the main source of income and one in six (16%) having welfare as the primary source. Twenty percent had a head or spouse 62 years of age or older and presumably relied on Social Security and/or pensions for income. Average rent paid by households was $259 per month. Government spending per unit averaged $331 a month.

Results

In operation, the program financed the construction or rehabilitation of projects containing more than 180,000 units, of which 114,000 were still available in 1998. Most projects now need rental assistance or other subsidy to cover a part of operating and maintenance costs. The one-time interest subsidy on development costs proved to be too shallow and had no built-in mechanism to deal with a situation of rising fuel and other operating costs

---

[34] Data in this section from *AHS: 1997*, and *A Picture of Subsized Households*, cited earlier.

and sluggish rent receipts from tenants with relatively fixed incomes, such as developed in the early 1970s. Nor did the program ever reach a scale to make a serious inroad into housing needs of low- and moderate-income families.

SECTION 236

This program was a major element in the Housing and Urban Development Act of 1968 (Public Law 90-448). It is an amendment to the National Housing Act, which authorizes various HUD-FHA mortgage insurance programs. Section 236 was intended to add substantially to the supply of rental and cooperative housing available to families with incomes above public housing limits in an area but insufficient for private market housing. For developers and investors, the returns and tax benefits were high, and activity was intense between 1969 and 1973. Difficulties associated with rising operating expenses in the early 1970s and lagging tenant incomes required operating subsidies for many of the projects. Although the program was replaced by other subsidized production programs, there were still 447,000 units available in 1998.

How the Program Worked

Section 236 was designed to provide new and rehabilitated housing for lower income families by reducing debt service costs. Eligible sponsors (owners) were nonprofit organizations such as churches and labor unions, cooperatives, and for-profit entities who agreed to a limited return of 6% on their equity. Periodic payments are made to lenders on behalf of the sponsor to reduce payments on the project mortgage to that required for principal, interest, and mortgage insurance premium on a loan bearing an interest of 1% for a term up to 40 years. A tenant or cooperative member initially paid the greater of a basic rent or 25% of income up to the charges necessary absent any interest reduction payments. The basic rent is equal to operating expenses plus amortization of the mortgage at 1%. Rents are regulated by the federal agency.

The process of getting sponsors, limited partners, and lending institutions together and gaining HUD-FHA approval was somewhat cumbersome, but was facilitated by builders, lawyers, and others. FHA personnel had the message from then-HUD Secretary George Romney to move expeditiously on applications, and they did.

Who are Served

Initially, the program enrolled families with a median income in 1971 of $5,000, or roughly $20,000 in 1999 dollars. The income range was between $17,000 and $28,000 in 1999 dollars, depending upon location and size of household. In 1998, average (somewhat higher than median) household income was $11,000. Those residing in projects without additional subsidies had incomes averaging $13,000 a year, occupants in the much larger group of projects receiving additional subsidies had an average income of $10,000 in 1998. Almost two in five (37%) reported wages as the main source of income, welfare for one in eight (12%). Average monthly rent for these households was $261, almost matched by government spending at $253 per household. Rent was considerably higher ($379) and government spending much lower ($72) for households in projects with no additional subsidies.[35]

In 1998, one-parent families with children comprised 37 of all Section 236 households, those 62 years of age or older 34%. Households under age 62 with a disabled head or spouse made up 14%. There were smaller proportions of elderly, nonelderly disabled, and one-person families with children in the projects not receiving additional subsidies.

Minorities constituted more than half of all households including blacks (36%), Hispanics (13%), Asians or Pacific Islanders (5%), and Native Americans (1%).

Results

The program was heavily applied for by builders operating through limited-return companies; these accounted for about two-thirds of approved projects, nonprofit groups and cooperatives about one-third. Inducements included accelerated depreciation allowances which offered a high annual return in the early years to limited partners; the deep interest rate reduction could lower rents by as much as one-third below rents of comparables built at market mortgage interest rates, promising a strong demand; and in some cases builders got site costs approved at substantially more than the price recently paid. By 1973, projects with units totaling about 450,000 units had FHA fund reservations or obligations of contract authority, and most of the units were available for subsidy payment within the following two to three years.

---

[35] Data in this section from *AHS: 1997*.

As with the earlier BMIR program, Section 236 had no built-in mechanism for dealing with rising fuel and maintenance expenses. A limited percentage of Section 236 families received an additional rent supplement subsidy, but most project owners were not prepared for the spurt in fuel and other operating expenses associated with the oil embargo of 1973. It thus became necessary to provide additional subsidies if the projects were to remain solvent. In 1998, 87% of the 447,000 units still available in Section 236 projects relied upon additional subsidies like Section 8.

In 1973, the Nixon Administration suspended a number of housing programs including Section 236. A housing policy review concluded that Section 236 was inefficient. Among other reasons, HUD's review team found that "Federal costs are higher than the value of the housing provided and because the tenant places a lower value on the transfer in-kind benefit than on an unrestricted cash grant." The same criticism can be made of most in-kind benefit programs by market-oriented analysts, partly because benefits to the rest of society are difficult to measure.

In any event, the Section 236 program was essentially replaced by the Section 8 New Construction and Substantial Rehabilitation program authorized in 1974, discussed below.

SECTION 8 NEW CONSTRUCTION AND SUBSTANTIAL REHABILITATION

Building new housing directly for low- and moderate-income residents was the standard approach prior to the 1970s. But as the general supply of housing expanded and doubts were raised about the cost effectiveness of new construction, lawmakers were attracted by the idea of utilizing existing housing to shelter the poor. A major overhaul of housing laws in 1974 included both approaches — a project-based new construction/substantial rehabilitation program and a rent certificate program for use in existing housing — both known as Section 8.

More than 15,000 projects were built under this program before authority to undertake additional contracts was repealed as of October 1983. An exception was made for new housing developments for the elderly and persons with disabilities financed under a small program known as Section 202 (and later, for a similar but separately funded Section 811 program for persons with disabilities). In 1998 894,000 units containing 1.4 million people were still under contract for Section 8 project-based assistance. Within the total, about 224,000 units were financed under Section 202 housing for the elderly and 18,000 units financed under Section 811 housing for persons with disabilities.

How the Program Works

HUD contracts directly for such developments with private owners or state or local agencies. The legislation authorized payment contracts with private owners for up to 20 years arid 40 years for projects owned or financed by a state or local agency. Payment contracts are adjusted periodically to allow for increases in cost of heat and other utilities, maintenance, and other operating expenses. Owners select low-income applicants based on HUD admission criteria. Under 1998 legislation, 40% of units becoming available must be assigned to households with extremely low incomes (under 30% of area median income), and 75% to 85% of openings must be assigned to households with incomes less than 50% of area median income. The purpose is to offset at least partially the targeting under the same law to somewhat higher income households to be admitted to public housing.

Who are Served

In 1998, 60% of residents were older persons (head of household or spouse age 62 or older). In the projects produced without Section 202 financing, 47% of the households were elderly. Disabled persons under 62 years of age occupied at least 17% of all units in this program. Fewer than one in four households (23%) contained children under 18 years of age.

Thirty-five percent were African American or Hispanic, lower than the percentages in public housing (66%) and the Section 8 certificate/voucher program (55%).

Relatively few (7%) reported welfare as their main source of income, but many were probably receiving Social Security or Supplemental Security Income payments. Average household income was $9,100. Residents paid, on average, $196 a month for rent and utilities. The federal government's expenditure per unit averaged $493 per month.

Issues

As noted, authority to subsidize new or substantially rehabilitated projects under this program was revoked in 1983 with the exception of a small volume of developments for elderly or disabled persons. Still, the program provides affordable housing to about three-quarters of a million households, many of whom are elderly or disabled. There is concern that many projects and apartments will be lost as owners with expiring contracts choose to leave the program; many other projects and units could be lost through default and foreclosure as a result of rising operating costs.

Mark-to-Market Program

Over the years, rents in some FHA-insured projects with Section 8 assistance have risen above going rents in the unsubsidized rental housing sector, due in part to virtually automatic rent adjustments by HUD. Since tenants paid a percentage of relatively fixed incomes, the increasing costs were largely borne by the federal government. About 850,000 units are in projects with mortgages insured by FHA. If the Section 8 subsidies were to be cut, owners might default on their mortgages, so savings in one program would be offset by losses in another, the FHA multifamily insurance fund. To address this situation, a portfolio reengineering program called "mark-to-market" was approved in 1997 as part of the FY1998 Appropriations Act. HUD estimates that ending excessive subsidies to private owners will save taxpayers almost $1.6 billion over five years.

Under mark-to-market, mortgage debt is to be written down on FHA-insured projects receiving Section 8 project-based subsidies to levels sustainable by street rents; a low-interest rate (soft) second mortgage is provided for the difference between the old loan balance and the amount of the new or restructured first mortgage. Costs will be charged against an FHA insurance fund. Owners have the option of participating, but the markdowns will not be available for properties that have seriously deteriorated due to mismanagement or where an owner has misused federal subsidies or engaged in fraud. In the case of poor maintenance, however, HUD could give an owner the chance to correct conditions or could even transfer the property to a qualified owner such as a tenant organization. The new owner would then be eligible to seek debt restructuring.[36]

---

[36] See CRS Report 97-1002 E, *HUD Multifamily Housing Reform: Section 8 Restructuring*, November 10, 1997, by Susan Vanhorenbeck.

How many owners will volunteer to have their mortgages written down will partly depend upon tax considerations. Legislators recognized, when approving the program, that the tax code generally treats cancellation of debt as taxable income. Conferees called upon the tax-writing committees to consider changes in law to overcome owner reluctance to participate for tax reasons. This problem may now largely be resolved by a ruling of the Internal Revenue Service.[37]

The portfolio reengineering is being carried out with the help of Participating Administrative Entities (PAEs), primarily state and local housing finance agencies. For a fee, these PAEs examine individual projects for condition, management performance, and rents, and recommend rent reductions with or without debt restructuring. HUD makes final decisions on PAE recommendations. At this writing, rent reductions had been effected without the need for debt restructuring (market-to-market lite) for 30 projects. About 1,000 deals were in process, of which 55% were "lite" and the others requiring debt restructuring.

Appropriations

The FY2000 HUD appropriation provides $10.8 billion for expiring Section 8 contracts, of which roughly one-third is for renewal of contracts with owners of Section 8 new and rehabilitation projects and other assisted projects.

HUD anticipated that some owners of well-located subsidized properties that can command market rents for comparable unsubsidized apartments would choose to drop out of the program when their Section 8 contracts expire, and their low-income tenants forced to move. The fiscal year 1999 appropriation included $433.5 million that could be tapped to provide tenant protection vouchers and moving expenses to such displaced households. The corresponding set-aside in the FY2000 appropriation is $156 million.

The FY2000 appropriation Act, however, seeks to minimize opt-outs of Section 8 contracts by providing for below-market Section 8 rents to be raised to market levels upon the renewal of a contract. In those situations where an opt-out still occurs, the tenants are protected by "enhanced

---

[37] A ruling by the Internal Revenue Service (98-34) issued July 21, 1998 holds that the Original Issue Discount (OID) rules will not apply to the use of soft second mortgages in the mark-to-market program, thus avoiding cancellation of indebtedness income because of OID. However, other tax pitfalls may still be present. See Housing and Development Reporter, *Current Developments,* July 27, 1998, p. 163.

vouchers" to allow them to remain in a project with HUD subsidizing the market rent.

THE LOW-INCOME HOUSING TAX CREDIT

While HUD's authority to provide assistance for new construction or substantial rehabilitation was essentially revoked in 1983, another window was opened in 1986 through the tax code, the Low Income Housing Tax Credit program (LIHTC). Over a 13-year period 700,000 to 800,000 units have been produced through this program.

How the Program Works

Under LIHTC, tax credits are allocated to each state on the basis of population. State housing finance agencies award the credits on a competitive basis to sponsors of developments for low-income people. In turn, sponsors, through financial intermediaries, sell tax credits to investors, both individuals and corporations, who may have no particular interest in housing *per se*. Investors apply these tax credits against unrelated income over a period of 10 years. For new construction, the tax credits provide 70% of the cost of development; for projects financed with tax-exempt bonds, 30%.

Proceeds from the sale of tax credits are used by sponsors — four fifths of whom are for profit, one fifth nonprofit – as equity capital and to reduce the amount of long-term debt. Sponsors must arrange long-term financing through other sources, such as FHA-insured loans, Rural Housing Service loans at interest rates as low as 1%, or tax-exempt bonds issued by state or local housing finance agencies. Local jurisdictions may help reduce needed capital funds with federal funds received through community development block grants and HOME grant money. Local contributions by some jurisdictions may include real estate tax abatement. Rental subsidies to cover a portion of operating expenses have also been obtained through Section 8.

The tax credit alone lowers rents by perhaps 20% to 30% below market rents on new apartments. It takes one or more other subsidies, along with the tax credit to bring the rents down to a level affordable by extremely low-income families.

The LIHTC is under the general oversight of the Internal Revenue Service, which may retroactively revoke tax credits for projects where sponsors have failed to enforce tenant income limits or comply with other requirements. Operating responsibility is vested in state and local housing finance agencies. These agencies receive an annual allocation of $1.25 per resident of the state. Thus, a state with a population of 5 million could get $6.25 million a year in tax credits to distribute to applicants. An association representing the housing finance agencies estimates that more than one million dwellings have been produced through this program from 1987 through 1997; others place the volume at 700,000 to 800,000 units. The revenue loss (tax expenditure) to the federal government in fiscal year 2000 is estimated at $4 billion; over four years 2000-2003, revenue forgone is projected at $18.4 billion.[38]

Who are Served

The law provides that 20% of the units in a tax credit project be assigned to families with incomes at or below 50% of area median income or 40% of units to families with incomes at or below 60% of area median. In fact, most projects are occupied by quite low income households — 37% with 1996 incomes below 30% of area median income and 76% below 50% of area median in projects put in service between 1992 and 1994, according to the U.S. General Accounting Office. Average income was $13,300. In 1996, 27% of households in tax-credit units benefited from project-based rental assistance and 12% had tenant-based assistance, but most got no rental assistance.

Small households of one or two persons occupy about two-thirds of all units, but there were more young household heads (44% under age 35) than older heads (29% 55 or older). Three-fifths (62%) of the households were headed by a woman, 35% were male-headed, the other 3% not known. More than half were white households, one-third were black, 11% Hispanic.[39]

---

[38] Based on estimates of tax expenditures prepared for the House Committee on Ways and Means and the Senate Committee on Finance by the Staff of the Joint Committee on Taxation, 1998. For additional information on the LIHTC program, see CRS RS20337, *The Low Income Housing Tax Credit: Current Issues and Proposed Legislation,* by Richard Bourdon, updated December 21, 1999.

[39] *Tax Credits: Opportunities to Improve Oversight of the Low-Income Housing Program,* Report to the Chairman, Committee on Ways and Means; and the Chairman, Subcommittee on Oversight, Committee on Ways and Means, House of Representatives, by the United States General Accounting Office, March 1997, pp. 38-42.

Issues

Analysts have raised questions about the efficiency of the program in lowering rents for low-income tenants. There are substantial front-end costs in the form of syndicating and underwriting fees, legal expenses, developers' fees and other charges that are paid out before the proceeds from the tax credit can be applied to rent reduction. These costs are thought to be coming down because of strong investor demand for such credits. But some professionals estimate syndication-related costs at 20% and total leakage at up to 30% when developers' profit is included. Some analysts contend that grants for reducing capital costs of such developments would be less expensive than tax credits. But tax credits are more likely to be approved by Congress than appropriations for grants.

Because the subsidies are heavily front-end, limited partners have less and less incentive to see that the property is properly maintained as their tax credits near expiration, despite the possibility that a portion of the credits may have to be paid back if the project is sold or fails to qualify for low-income use within 15 years.

The General Accounting Office found that some state allocating agencies could do a better job in controlling project costs, including obtaining more reliable verification of cost and financing data submitted by developers, and monitoring projects for compliance with program requirements.[40]

Legislation

Advocacy groups backed a proposal, supported by the Clinton Administration, to raise the annual allocation from $1.25 to $1.75 per resident of each state. This would have made it possible to finance an additional 100,000 or more units a year compared with 75,000 a year in recent years. The proposal failed to be enacted in 1998 or in 1999. The Clinton Administration has renewed its support for raising the cap on the LIHTC from $1.25 to $1.75 per capita starting in calendar 2001 and indexing the cap for inflation in each year thereafter. This would raise the cost in forgone revenues from $4 billion to $5 billion a year.

---

[40] *Ibid.*, pp. 8-12.

THE HOME INVESTMENT PARTNERSHIPS PROGRAM (HOME)

This program, the centerpiece of the National Affordable Housing Act of 1990, focuses on rehabilitation, construction and acquisition of housing for low-income families, both renters and owners. The program is administered by the Department of Housing and Urban Development.

How the Program Works

Grants are distributed by formula to state and local governments. After a 0.2% set-aside for Insular Areas, 60% of HOME funds is allocated to metropolitan cities, urban counties, and consortia of contiguous local governments; states get 40%. Participating jurisdictions must prepare and gain HUD's approval of a plan that identifies housing needs and strategies to meet these needs. Jurisdictions must put up a matching grant of 25 cents for each dollar of HOME funds expended. Acceptable sources of matching funds include taxes and fees forgone, value of donated real estate, bond financing, and donated construction materials and volunteer labor; CDBG and other federal funds are not eligible for matching. Local matching requirements may be partially or wholly waived by HUD for jurisdictions in fiscal distress or severe fiscal distress or in places declared disaster areas by the President.

For the most part, HOME funds are blended with funds from other sources such as low-income housing tax credits or community development block grants to bring homes or apartments within the means of assisted families. HUD staff view HOME funds as a form of "gap" assistance that makes feasible projects that need some additional subsidy. They estimate that each federal dollar of HOME funds leverages at least $2.40 from other sources.

Given wide latitude in planning HOME activities, many local jurisdictions have chosen to strengthen ownership: home purchasers are prominent among indicated beneficiaries, and together with incumbent homeowners account for 56% of committed units. However, when tenant-based rental assistance is included, rentals account for 50% of units and 56% of HOME funds committed.

An objective of the statute is to encourage development by Community Housing Development Organizations (CHDOs). These are private, community-based nonprofit organizations established under state or local laws to provide affordable housing to low- and moderate income persons. Participating jurisdictions receiving HOME funds are required to reserve at least 15% of the money for housing to be sponsored, developed or owned by CHDOs. Cumulatively, about one-fifth of committed HOME funds have been reserved for CHDOs.

Who are Served

In general, at least 90% of families assisted in rental housing with some HOME funds must have incomes not exceeding 60% of area median income, and the other 10% with incomes below 80% of area median income. Rental projects must have rents that are the lesser of the existing Fair Market Rent or 30% of the adjusted rent of a family whose income is 65% of median area income. Incomes of benefiting homebuyers or existing owners cannot exceed 80% of median area income.

The outcomes, in terms of rent burdens, are mixed. A preponderance (84%) of assisted renter households in completed HOME projects had incomes below 50% of median area income, and more than two in five (44%) had extremely low incomes (30% of area median or less). But most of the extremely low income renters without additional tenant-based rental assistance had rents greater than 30% of income, and two in five were paying over 50%.[41]

Families who bought homes through the HOME program were generally better off than renters. All had to have incomes below 80% of area median income, more than half (54%) had incomes below 60% of median income, and a third (32%) had incomes below 50% of median income. Homeowners who fixed up their properties with the help of HOME funds were closer to renters in terms of income: 69% of them had incomes below 50% of area median income and almost a third (31%) of assisted homeowners had extremely low incomes.

Issues

One issue has to do with the difficulty of serving the very poorest households through HOME or any housing subsidy program absent additional rental assistance. In HOME rental projects, the rents are flat or

---

[41] Sources are HOME program data from the U.S. Department of Housing and Urban Development, Office of Community Planning and Development, dated 11/29/99 and 1/28/00; rent burdens are those shown in an April 1998 HUD publication, *Rental Housing Assistance – The Crisis Continues,* cited earlier, pp. 28-29.

fixed and tenants without rental assistance pay the flat rent whatever their actual income. As noted, most extremely low income renters without additional rental assistance were paying more than 30% of income for housing. Another issue has to do with the effectiveness of housing counseling services provided with HOME funds. In connection with the FY2000 appropriation, congressional conferees reiterated the prior year's warning that HUD must establish and implement a process for measuring the performance of such housing counseling services.[42]

Accomplishments

In 1999, there were 589 jurisdictions participating in the HOME program. From 1992, when the program got under way, through September 1999, funds to produce or rehabilitate 465,000 units had been committed and 267,000 units completed. Almost half (49%) of the committed units are being rehabilitated, about a fourth (24%) are new construction, and more than a fourth (27%) are for acquisition of existing units. In terms of committed dollars, new construction has taken a disproportionate share (31%), rehabilitation close to its unit share (52%), and acquisition of existing standard housing relatively less (13%). Only a small proportion of the money (3.6%) has gone for tenant-based rental assistance.

Appropriations

The HOME program has an appropriation of $1.6 billion for fiscal year 2000, the same as the previous year. Net of administrative expenses by participating jurisdictions and community groups, about $1.4 billion is available for housing production. This amount is projected by HUD staff to fund about 89,000 units of rehabilitated, newly built, or acquired standard houses for low-income families and to provide tenant-based rental assistance to more than 10,000 low-income households. Within the total appropriation, $15 million is earmarked for housing counseling.

---

[42] House Report 106-379, October 13, 1999, pp. 116-117.

Chapter 4

USING THE EXISTING INVENTORY OF HOUSING

SECTION 8 RENT CERTIFICATES AND VOUCHERS

Academic studies and field tests funded by Congress indicated that it would be less expensive and would widen choices for low-income consumers to use existing housing rather than to build new developments.[43] Needy families would get certificates which they could use to rent space in the private rental housing market. This approach, known as Section 8 rent certificates, was adopted in 1974. Rent certificates, and a variant called vouchers introduced in 1983, now assist more families than any other housing program for low-income persons. In 1998, about 1.4 million households were receiving rent subsidies under this program. In addition, 108,000 households occupied moderately rehabilitated dwellings with the help of project-based Section 8 certificates.

How the Program Works

The program is administered at the local level by the public housing agency or another designated agency. The local agency is responsible for screening applicants and determining their eligibility, applying essentially the same criteria as for public housing applicants. Families receiving vouchers look for a place in the private rental market or may remain in their

---

[43] *The Experimental Housing Allowance Program: Conclusions, the 1980 Report,* U.S. Department of Housing and Urban Development, Government Printing Office, 1980.

present dwelling if it meets standards. The unit must be in acceptable condition as determined by an inspection. Under the earlier certificate program, the family paid 30% of adjusted income for rent, the certificate covering the balance of the rent specified in the assistance payment contract signed by the property owner and the PHA. The contract rent could not exceed a federally-determined fair market rent (FMR) for the area by more than 10%, 20% in certain circumstances. FMRs for each urban area are set periodically by HUD staff, and vary by number of bedrooms. The 1974 legislation authorized payment contracts with owners of existing units for as long as 15 years. Currently, payment contracts are limited to one year, but may be renewed subject to availability of federal funds.

In the case of vouchers, the family could pay more than 30% of income for rent to get a better dwelling, but the subsidy is never more than a "standard payment" which is based on the FMR at the initial date of the agreement. The PHA may allow annual rent adjustments (originally, only two rent increases to a landlord within a five year period). The PHA must find that the rent charged a tenant with a voucher is reasonable and that the family is spending a reasonable portion of its income for rent. These "reasonable" requirements evidently have not been uniformly enforced since a substantial number of voucher-receiving families have been found to be paying a rent in excess of 50% of income. Under the 1998 housing reform act, upon initial occupancy a family receiving tenant-based assistance may not be required to pay for rent more than 40% of its monthly adjusted income.

Who are Served

Households served by the Section 8 program are typically single parents with children under 18 years of age (56%). Elderly households (62 or older) comprise only one-sixth of recipients. Most participants have incomes below the poverty threshold; average household income is $9,600. Thirty-two percent report wages, business, or both as their main source of income, while welfare (TANF formerly known as AFDC, and General Assistance) is the main source for 21%. For others, the main sources of income are pensions, Social Security, Supplemental Security Income (for disabled persons and some elderly), unemployment benefits, child support, or mixtures.

Rent and utility payments by these households averaged $217 per month in 1998; the federal expenditure on their behalf averaged $471 per month. The smaller Section 8 moderate rehabilitation program accommodates households with poverty-level incomes (average of $7,800), although more than one-fourth derive most of their income from wages. These families paid an average monthly rent of $167 and federal spending per unit averaged $547.

How much Dispersion?

One of the arguments for rent certificates and vouchers is that recipients can choose to live outside of heavy concentrations of poverty and in racially diversified neighborhoods. In fact, dispersion of the poor and minority recipients through certificates and vouchers has occurred only to a limited degree, in part because "some stayed in place [while] others moved, but not far."[44] Holders of certificates and vouchers typically live in modest neighborhoods (only 20% of households in surrounding census tracts are below the poverty line and 40% in these tracts are single-family owners) and where two-fifths of all residents in the census tracts are minority households.

Challenges to this Program

To deal with poverty-related problems, some market-oriented economists and others argue for straight income transfers rather than in-kind assistance like rent vouchers. Satisfaction is presumably maximized if low-income beneficiaries can spend their money according to their own consumer preferences. In the same vein, it is reasoned that tenant-based housing assistance is preferable to project-based subsidies in that recipients can function like other consumers in the housing market.

But is the housing supply large enough to accommodate all renter households living in severely inadequate or crowded conditions, disregarding income or other limiting factors? A computer simulation of rental markets in 25 metropolitan areas found an insufficiency of standard dwellings in all areas studied.[45] Admittedly, this finding is based on a comparison of housing supply and need at one point in time, and it is possible that a substantial and sustained volume of tenant-based subsidies will induce an expansion of the available supply over a period of time. But

---

[44] Paul Burke, *A Picture of Subsidized Households in 1998*, HUD, August 28, 1998.
[45] For the full analysis, see *Existing Housing Resources vs. Need*, CRS Report 87-81 E, by Grace Milgram and Robert Bury, Congressional Research Service, January 30, 1987.

the study suggests that vouchers are not the total answer, and that some additional assisted housing production or rehabilitation will also be needed.

In practice, in many areas, families are "unable to utilize effectively this [tenant-based] housing subsidy," according to the Conference Report on HUD's FY2000 appropriation, "especially in high-cost areas where the payment standard of the voucher program may not be sufficient to cover market rents."[46] In tight markets, owners are unwilling to accept voucher holders because they do not want to discourage occupancy by households who can afford market rents without subsidy nor do they want to be monitored by government agencies. Moreover, the families themselves, over half of whom are African American (40%) or Hispanic (15%), may find it difficult to move outside of familiar territory. Commonly, they find accommodations in properties owned by landlords who specialize in subsidized rentals and list with the public housing agency.

Legislative Changes in 1998

Reluctance of landlords to rent to voucher holders may be partly due to the way the program was structured and administered prior to 1996. For one thing, landlords were subject to a rule of "take one — take all." If the owner of a multifamily building rented to one Section 8 tenant, he could not refuse to rent to other Section 8 applicants, even in other projects. Another factor was the "endless lease;" a landlord could not terminate a lease with a Section 8 tenant except for good cause. Both provisions were repealed by language inserted in appropriations acts each year beginning in FY1996. These requirements are permanently removed by the Quality Housing and Work Responsibility Act of 1998.

An important change in 1998 merges the Section 8 certificate and voucher programs with a payment standard of 90% to 110% of the fair market rent. As noted, when a family initially receives a voucher, it may not pay a rent greater than 40% of adjusted income. This is a much higher rent-to-income ratio than housing laws once deemed bearable by low-income families.

Another provision makes it easier for a tenant to move into a different PHA's jurisdiction and retain its voucher (portability). At the option of the public agency administering the program, a family may be allowed to use its voucher to make payments on a dwelling purchased by a member of the

---

[46] House Report 106-379, October 13, 1999, p. 89

family. This is consonant with other efforts to encourage low-income renters to become homeowners.

Appropriations

Appropriations were sufficient to renew expiring contracts from 1995 to 1998, but no funds for additional assisted units were provided during this period. The appropriations act for 1999 included $283 million for 50,000 new units for families moving from welfare to work. The FY2000 appropriation provides $10.8 billion to renew expiring contracts and $346.56 million to enable 60,000 incremental households to receive vouchers (not linked to welfare to work families).

Advocates have voiced concern that certificates or vouchers for those on the current rolls are being funded one year at a time. Without multiyear funding, contracts with private owners are limited to one year. This may discourage some property owners from participating; it also makes it more costly for local agencies to administer the program. But even with one-year funding, the cost (budget authority) of renewing all Section 8 contracts is projected to mount each year from $9.6 billion in 1999 to $16.5 billion in 2003.[47]

HOMEOWNERSHIP AND OPPORTUNITY FOR PEOPLE EVERYWHERE (HOPE)

The idea of enabling public housing tenants to become owners of their own apartments has found its way into legislation for at least 30 years. The Housing and Urban Development Act of 1968 permitted public housing authorities to buy leased properties with the purpose of reselling them to residents. Sales contracts were drawn on roughly 14,000 units, with final sales to about 2,000 families. A provision in the 1974 housing act permitted public housing authorities to sell projects to low-income tenants while continuing to receive annual payments to cover debt service on bonds issued to build the projects. Sales contracts were drawn on about 3,000 units.

---

[47] The increased budget authority is for 1.7 million units under contracts expiring in 1998 and increasing to 2.8 million units in 2003. Renewals of contracts, in dollars and units, include Section 8 new construction and rehabilitation, moderate rehabilitation, loan management, property disposition, and preservation units. Source: *HUD Budget Justification for FY1999*, Housing Certificate Fund (including contract renewals).

Legislation in 1987 authorized public housing authorities to help a resident council take steps toward acquiring a project for eventual ownership by tenants or other eligible low-income families. Proponents argued that as owners, residents of public housing would take better care of the properties, try to become more economically self-sufficient, and gain in self-esteem.

In 1990, the Bush Administration secured inclusion of this concept in the National Affordable Housing Act under the title Home Ownership and Opportunity for People Everywhere (HOPE). HOPE 1 was applicable to public and Indian housing projects. A similar program, called HOPE 2, was authorized for assisted or insured multifamily developments owned or held by HUD, USDA, and other federal agencies or determined by HUD to be financially or physically troubled. HOPE 3 permitted the sale of government-owned single-family houses to low-income families. Both planning grants and implementation grants were authorized. Implementation grants could cover property rehabilitation costs as well as counseling and training of purchasers. Implementation grants had to be matched by recipients — 25% in the case of HOPE 1 — a requirement that could be reduced or waived by HUD under a 1992 amendment. HOPE 3 initially required a 33% match of the federal implementation grant amount from non-federal sources, but this was reduced to 25% for subsequent grantees in the final two years.

The sale of public housing to resident groups proved difficult to implement. Planning grants were made for 231 projects, implementation grants for 30 projects. Sales agreements cover an estimated 2,900 units. High rehabilitation costs relative to appraised values of dwellings drew media attention, as with a 480-unit project in Washington DC named Kenilworth-Parkside. Like other HOPE projects, Kenilworth-Parkside is still owned by a resident management corporation which has yet to transfer ownership to occupants. HOPE 1 was de-emphasized by the Clinton Administration. No funds were appropriated for this program after Fiscal year 1995.

HOPE 2 was also discontinued after several years. According to HUD records, 13 multifamily projects containing a total of 2,689 units were sold to low-income tenants under this provision. Administrators recall that the properties had to be held in inventory by HUD for lengthy planning periods, during which time the properties might have been sold to other bidders. Some question whether it was appropriate to encourage people with little experience in real estate ownership to buy apartments, especially those which had been poorly built to begin with or were poorly located.

The sale of government-repossessed single-family properties under HOPE 3 has also been cumbersome. The properties must first be sold to nonprofit groups which then sell them to eligible families, a time-consuming process. The last round of HOPE 3 grants was awarded in FY1995. A total of 1,234 families became first-time homeowners through the program.

The HOPE programs were too short-lived to develop much of a track record.

Advocates promoted the approach in the belief that homeownership by itself brings a discernible, positive transformation in work and family behavior patterns of low-income renters and thereby benefits society. Empirical support for this view is lacking. In one recent study, analysts concluded: "The many arguments for extending homeownership opportunities to the poor that rest on claims that the extension will produce social benefits that will improve American society seem to us to rest on shaky grounds, if any."[48]

Sale of Public Housing under 1998 Act

Despite limited results in earlier efforts, the idea of selling public and assisted housing to low-income households retains a place in the panoply of federal housing programs. The 1998 Act includes a provision that allows local housing agencies to sell public and other acquired housing to low-income families for use as a primary residence, but with limitations upon economic gains from early resale. Current residents have the right of first refusal. Those who choose not to buy and are displaced will receive vouchers for use in comparable but standard housing, relocation expenses, counseling, and other protections.

---

[48] Peter H. Rossi and Eleanor Weber, "The Social Benefits of Homeownership: Empirical Evidence from National Surveys," Fannie Mae Annual Housing Conference, 1995.

Chapter 5

HOUSING FOR SPECIAL POPULATIONS

HOUSING FOR THE ELDERLY AND NON-ELDERLY DISABLED

In 1959, Congress authorized a direct loan program (Section 202) to provide rental housing and related facilities for the elderly. Handicapped persons and their families were made eligible in 1964. The projects, new or rehabilitated structures, could include dining facilities, community rooms, infirmaries, and other service facilities. Initially, only nonprofit sponsors could avail themselves of the loans, but in 1961 consumer cooperatives and some public bodies were made eligible. Over a period of time, the interest rate was kept at or close to 3% to reduce rents for those who might not be able to afford apartments built at market rents. Loans initially could cover up to 98%, later 100%, of total development cost and have a pay-out term of up to 50 years. (An FHA market-rate program, Section 231, was also adopted in 1959 to insure, loans for rental housing for elderly who could afford market rents.)

In the early 1970s, utility and maintenance costs rose while incomes of elderly residents lagged and rents were insufficient to cover operating expenses. Rental assistance through Section 8 was made available in 1974. In 1990, Section 8 subsidies were replaced by operating cost subsidies specific to Section 202 projects. Assistance payments are set to keep tenants' contribution for rent and utilities to roughly 30% of monthly adjusted income. In recognition of the needs of elderly residents, funds may now be used not only for constructing service facilities but for providing supportive services within the facilities.[49]

The 1990 Act also changed the method of financing. For projects developed after September, 1991, direct loans were replaced by no-interest capital advances that are forgiven (in effect grants) if affordability requirements are complied with for 40 years. Only private, nonprofit organizations with experience in housing or related social service activities are eligible to receive a capital advance.

Problems

The admission of persons with disabilities posed a difficulty. Lifestyles of the disabled, it became clear, differed from those of most elderly residents. In 1988, HUD was instructed by Congress to establish procedures for separating units for the non-elderly disabled from apartments for the elderly. Two years later, Congress authorized a separate source of funds for persons with disabilities under Section 811 of the National Affordable Housing Act of 1990. In 1992, so-called mixed population legislation restricted the occupancy of non-elderly disabled persons in public housing and privately-owned HUD subsidized projects for the elderly.

The biggest general problem, of course, is that these programs for the elderly and the non-elderly disabled can assist only a small fraction of the populations eligible for such housing and services. In 1998, Section 202-financed projects contained about 224,000 units, all with rental assistance. For non-elderly with disabilities, there were about 18,000 units. HUD estimates that in 1995 almost 1.5 million elderly persons were in households with worst-case needs (paying more than one-half their income for rent or living in severely substandard dwellings). Adults with disabilities in worst-case needs households numbered between 1.1 and 1.4 million households.[50] Current levels of assistance would have to be expanded considerably to make substantial inroads into these housing problems. The frail elderly, largely those 85 years of age and older, are projected to make up an increasing proportion of the elderly with special housing requirements.

---

[49] For more detailed discussions, see CRS Report 93-645 E, *Evolution of Section 202; Housing for the Elderly,* by Susan Vanhorenbeck, revised June 23, 1993; and CRS Report 94-177 E, *Rental Assistance for the Disabled,* February 28, 1994, by Susan Vanhorenbeck.

[50] Data on housing-disadvantaged renter elderly and nonelderly households with disabilities from *Waiting in Vain,* cited above, p. 1.

Appropriations

HUD's FY2000 appropriation includes $710 million for Section 202 housing for the elderly, an increase of $50 million over the 1999 budget. In the past, funds have been used for capital advances, project rental assistance, and supportive services associated with the housing. The FY2000 appropriation does not provide funds for any capital repairs, but earmarks $50 million for conversion of existing projects for the elderly to assisted living facilities. Such facilities provide more intensive services than traditional housing for the elderly can provide, and recognizes a growing proportion of frail elderly. Another $50 million is earmarked for service coordinators and existing congregate service grants.

For Section 811 housing for persons with disabilities, $201 million is provided, an increase of $7 million over 1999. Funds may be used for purposes similar to those for elderly housing.

HOUSING FOR THE HOMELESS

The plight of individuals and families living in temporary quarters, on the streets, or on the road is not a new phenomenon; it goes back to the colonial period. But in recent decades, such individuals became more visible as cheap hotels and single-room occupancies were demolished and their occupants disgorged, state mental institutions were closed and their clients placed in the community, a drug epidemic swept parts of the city, and a changing economy left some families without steady work and rent-paying ability. In early 2000, at least 600,000 persons were homeless on any one night and perhaps 2.3 million persons would experience a period of homelessness at least once in the course of a year.

Program

The problem drew a response from Congress in 1987 with passage of the Stewart B. McKinney Homeless Assistance Act of that year. Under this law, grants are made to states, local governments, nonprofit organizations, and community mental health associations who agree to provide shelter and care for those without permanent housing. Grants may be made for emergency shelters, supportive services in transitional housing to facilitate movement to independent living, and permanent housing for handicapped homeless individuals. Funds provided for the emergency shelter program may be used to prevent homelessness of those facing loss of their homes due to a sudden drop in income. Contracts with providers are generally for ten years and require equal matching grants.

Single-room occupancies (SROs) can be funded for homeless persons under the Section 8 moderate rehabilitation program. HUD makes annual contributions to public housing agencies, which in turn contract with private owners for the rehabilitation and conversion of properties into single room dwellings. Rental assistance for SRO units is provided by HUD are for ten years. Supportive services are provided to the individual occupants along with rental assistance. There is no matching fund requirement for this program.

The National Affordable Housing Act of 1990 added a Shelter Plus Care program that permits HUD to provide rental assistance along with supportive services to homeless persons with mental disabilities, chronic drug or alcohol problems, or with AIDS. Help goes to units already assisted under Section 8 and other programs for special populations (repealed in 1992 in connection with, Section 202 housing for the elderly and Section 811 housing for the disabled).

Amendments in 1992 required recipients of McKinney Act funds to involve homeless individuals or families in arranging activities of the facility and to participate on the policy-making board. A demonstration program named "Safe Havens" was established to provide shelter for mentally ill persons who are currently unable or unwilling to take part in mental health or substance abuse treatment programs.[51]

In 1994, HUD initiated a new Continuum of Care approach in the distribution of competitively awarded funds for the homeless. Each locality is encouraged to prepare a comprehensive plan to meet housing and service needs of the homeless in the community, with broad participation of providers for the homeless, advocates, homeless persons, business groups, and others. Taking account of local circumstances, the community's application must address four elements of need: prevention, emergency shelter, transitional housing with supportive services, and permanent housing.

---

[51] For a more detailed account, see CRS Report 97-486 E, *Current Operation of HUD Homeless Assistance Programs,* April 24, 1997, by Pauline H. Smale; also, CRS Report 98-181 E, *H.R. 217: Homeless Housing Programs Consolidation and Flexibility Act,* March 2, 1998, by Pauline Smale.

Who are They?

Homeless individuals and families are a diverse group but have in common a lack of any financial resources. While some have seasonal or part-time jobs, many are unable to cope in the labor force. One-third or more of the homeless are believed to be mentally ill, persons who were "deinstitutionalized" from state mental institutions or never in hospitals because they were not deemed a threat to themselves or others. Others are alcoholics or substance abusers. Still others simply are without means to pay rent.

A survey released in 1999 based on 1996 data found that two in five homeless persons showed signs of mental illness and two-thirds suffered from chronic or infectious diseases (other than AIDS). More than one-fourth reported a childhood history of foster care or institutional placement.[52]

Families who are homeless differ little from similar poor families with permanent housing in terms of mental illness, substance abuse or crime. Lack of wherewithal to pay rent seems to be the main cause of family homelessness, along with domestic violence, or displacement by flooding, fire, or other disasters.[53]

In rural areas, homelessness is less visible than in urban places but not insignificant. Homeless people may be living in cars or campers or crowded in with relatives or friends. The rural homeless are more likely than those in urban areas to be working but poor families with children, and homeless for the first time.[54] They are most apt to be found in agricultural regions or in areas with declining extractive industries such as mining, fishing, or timber.

Issues

A continuing debate is over the priority to assign to the homeless. Does an increase in funding for the homeless come at the expense of less housing money for the elderly or public housing? This might be the case if the budget process requires an appropriations subcommittee with a fixed allocation to offset an increase in funding for one domestic program by cutting others.

---

[52] See *Homelessness: Programs and the People They Serve – Summary Report*, prepared by The Urban Institute for the Interagency Council on the Homeless, Washington, DC, December 1999, pp. xvii-xxii.
[53] *The New York Times*, December 5, 1999, pp. 41, 44.
[54] National Coalition for the Homeless, Fact Sheet #13, March 1999.

Further, once the funds are allocated to participating jurisdictions, should homeless families or individuals be put at the head of the line for housing assistance that many other poor families have been waiting to get for months or years? Under federal preferences until recently the homeless were placed at the head of the queue, but not all agree that this is fair. Public housing agencies are now permitted to set their own priorities, so the competition for limited assistance continues at the local level.

Another issue is recidivism: What happens to individuals after they "graduate" from the Continuum of Care program? How many will fall back into a condition requiring further treatment and assisted housing? Will supportive services again be available? A Census Bureau survey cited by HUD found that 60% of single adults move on to a better living situation after getting assistance. But what should be done with the other 40%?

Accomplishments

The Census Bureau survey noted above found that 76% of all homeless families move on to better living circumstances after receiving assistance. HUD states that about 400,000 people are no longer homeless, thanks to local efforts supported by its Continuum of Care program.

Appropriations

HUD's FY2000 appropriation for homeless assistance grants is $1.02 billion, an increase of $45 million over the 1999 appropriation. The funds are used for coordinated efforts to move homeless persons, including the mentally ill, through a continuum of care from temporary shelter to permanent housing, and for substance abuse treatment, job training, and restoration of dignity necessary for a return to independent living.

HOUSING OPPORTUNITIES FOR PERSONS WITH AIDS (HOPWA)

AIDS, acquired immunodeficiency syndrome, came to national attention in the 1980s, although the virus may have emerged in 1930. At the end of 1997 an estimated 247,000 persons in the United States were living with AIDS and an additional 500,000-800,000 persons were estimated to be living with HIV infection, the associated disease. New cases reported to the Centers for Disease Control and Prevention for the 12-month period ending March 1998 numbered more than 57,000 adults, adolescents, and children.

The Housing Opportunities for Persons with AIDS program (HOPWA) was enacted in 1990 as part of the Cranston-Gonzalez National Affordable Housing Act, and amended by the Housing and Community Development Act of 1992. Its purpose is to encourage states and localities to develop strategies and programs for meeting housing and supportive services needs of persons with HIV/AIDS and their families. An estimated 102-107 jurisdictions qualified for a formula allocation in FY2000.

How the Program Works

Grants are made to states and local jurisdictions, 90% by formula, the balance by competitive application for special projects of national significance or other projects. Grantees may use the funds for short-term rental assistance, to develop community residences for persons with AIDS, and for housing information and technical assistance to nonprofit organizations. Services may be provided both in the assisted facilities and independently of any housing activity. Services may include counseling, day care, nutritional services, and intensive care when required.

The assistance is designed to prevent homelessness of persons with AIDS and their families. Short-term rental assistance, whether project-based or tenant-based, is for low-income individuals, defined as those with incomes below 80% of area median income. No fees may be charged to low-income persons or families for any services provided with grant funds.

Who Benefits?

Clients who have received housing assistance through HOPWA were mostly at the lowest income levels with roughly 73% having family incomes of less than $500 a month and 96% with less than $1,000 per month.

Appropriations

HUD's FY2000 budget justification for this program noted that an increasing number of jurisdictions are eligible for this program and new cases are being added to those already served. Thus, there is growing demand for HOPWA funds. For fiscal year 2000, $232 million has been appropriated, an increase of $17 million over 1999. The appropriation is expected to support about 42,000 units of housing assistance and provide services to about 77,000 individuals. As in 1999, a preponderance of housing units and persons served is for short-term rent, mortgage and utility payments to prevent homelessness, and short-term facilities.

HOUSING FOR NATIVE AMERICANS THROUGH HUD

Native Americans on tribal lands and Alaskan villagers constitute a special population in rural areas. The proportion of families living below the poverty line is three times that of rural whites, unemployment is high, and economic prospects bleak. The unemployment rate on Indian reservations is about ten times the national average. For many, housing conditions are wretched: about 16% of households in Native American areas lack complete plumbing. The homeownership rate among Native Americans is only 30%, compared with 67% for all U.S. households, according to an advocacy group.[55]

Problems

The underlying problem for Native Americans in tribal areas is unemployment and underemployment. Some people work on farms, others are employed by the government, and tourism has brought some jobs. But lack of infrastructure such as roads, telephone lines and utilities and the thinness of markets translate into a weak economic base. These limitations, in turn, deter banks and other lending institutions from making residential and commercial loans in Native American areas.

A further complication is that land is held in trust for the tribal community. Lenders cannot collateralize a home loan when it is on communal property. Lenders cannot foreclose on properties sited on tribal land in the event of default on mortgage loans. Moreover, Native American residents do not want to see tribal land taken by outsiders. HUD, USDA and other agencies are trying to deal with these difficulties.[56]

---

[55] Estimated by Chester Carl, chairman, National American Indian Housing Council, Washington, DC, cited in CD publications, *Housing Affairs Letter,* November 5, 1999, p. 4.
[56] These problems are detailed in *Taking Stock of Rural Poverty and Housing for the 1990s,* cited earlier, p. 50.

Programs

The lead federal agency for Indian programs is the Bureau of Indian Affairs in the Department of the Interior, which attempts to coordinate various efforts like those of the Department of Housing and Urban Development.[57] HUD administers an Indian housing program similar to public housing with about 73,000 units. There are long waits for these units — 41 months on average. A high proportion of residents are families with children (70%). Residents of Indian housing have higher average incomes than public housing tenants ($17,000 versus $9,100). This apparently reflects a policy of selecting working families. Over half of tenants derive a majority of their income from wages or business.

A number of aids to Native Americans were combined into a Native American Housing Block Grant program in 1996. The rationale is that tribal governments need flexibility in use of funds since conditions vary from one tribal area to another. Grants may be used for new construction, rehabilitation of dwellings, operating subsidies, supportive services to residents, and counseling. These activities are expected to generate badly needed economic development. On the basis of plans prepared by tribal authorities, HUD began to make implementation grants in July 1998.

In addition, Native American entities have a set-aside within HUD's budget for community development block grants. These funds are mainly used for public works such as sewers and water facilities, as well as housing and economic development activities.

Appropriations

For fiscal year 2000, Native American housing block grants are funded at $620 million, the same level as in fiscal year 1999. This amount includes $6 million for technical assistance grants, $4 million for HUD and $2 million for the National American Indian Housing Council, a group with skills potentially useful in dealing with the special status of tribal reservation lands. The set-aside in FY2000 for the Native American CDBG program is $67 million, the same as in the previous year.

---

[57] Direct housing activities of the Bureau of Indian Affairs are limited to a small housing improvement program.

RURAL HOUSING

Housing problems of families in nonmetropolitan areas receive relatively little attention from the national media. Yet some of the most grinding poverty and housing deficiencies are located outside of cities and suburbs. About 4.3 million households in nonmetropolitan areas had incomes below the poverty line in 1997, including many female-headed families, children, and elderly.[58] Close to two million households in nonmetropolitan areas, including owners and renters, were paying 40% or more of income on shelter and utilities. The number of very-low-income renter households paying 50% or more of income for rent increased by 14% between 1991 and 1997. But severe and moderate physical problems, as defined by HUD, declined by about one-fourth in nonmetropolitan area between 1991 and 1997.

Programs

Federal programs to deal with non-urban housing needs are administered principally by the Rural Housing Service (RHS) — formerly the Farmers Home Administration — of the U.S. Department of Agriculture (USDA). The Bankhead-Jones Farm Tenant Act of 1937 authorized USDA to make long-term, low-interest rate loans to farm tenants and sharecroppers for the purchase and repair of farms, including homes on the farm. A 1946 Act established the Farmers Home Administration and amended Bankhead-Jones to give preference to veterans in direct loans for the purchase or improvement of farms and the insurance of loans made by private institutions for the same purposes.

Authority for the Farmers Home Administration to make loans to rural residents other than farmers was enacted in 1961. "Rural areas" were defined by administrators as open country and places rural in character with up to 2,500 residents. Today, such loans maybe made in places with up to 10,000 population and up to 20,000 if outside a metropolitan area when USDA and HUD find that the area has a serious lack of mortgage credit.

---

[58] Households below the poverty line from *AHS: 1997,* Census Bureau. Other information is drawn or updated from papers presented at a Fannie Mae Research Roundtable co-sponsored by the Housing Assistance Council and the California Coalition for Rural Housing Project, *A Home in the Country: The Housing Challenges Facing Rural America,* October 1995. The data presented in this section are for nonmetropolitan areas; if rural areas inside metropolitan areas were included, the numbers of households and dwellings would be substantially higher.

USDA home loans are intended to help families buy or repair modest houses. Applicants for direct loans must show that they have been unable to get loans elsewhere with their own resources or at reasonable terms. Direct loans to lower income families and individuals were authorized in 1968 (Section 502); loans could bear interest rates as low as one percent. Currently, such loans are targeted to families with incomes 80% of area median or less; within this group, 40% of the loans must go to those with very low-incomes (under 50% of area median income), 60% to families and individuals with incomes 50% to 80% of area median. A Section 502 loan guarantee for moderate-income home purchasers is also available and is increasingly emphasized as against direct loans. Families and individuals with incomes up to 115% of median income in the area are eligible to receive such loans.

USDA also is permitted to make loans for rental housing (Section 515) intended for lower income residents. Interest on loans for such projects may be as low as one percent. Project owners of some of these subsidized apartments sought to prepay their mortgages and put their apartments into the unsubsidized rental market. Inducements to keep the units for low-income tenants and restrictions on who could purchase these buildings were adopted in 1988. In October 1999, 452,366 units were available to lower income families at below-market rents made possible by the interest-reduced loans of the Section 515 rural housing program.

A rental assistance program (Section 521) similar to HUD's Section 8 rental assistance, discussed earlier, enables some very low-income families to afford USDA-financed rental housing. About 245,000 households were getting these deep subsidies in October 1999. Virtually all of these rent-assisted families were lodged in multifamily housing financed by USDA under the Section 515 program. In addition, about 45,000 families in these USDA developments were receiving project-based rental assistance through HUD's Section 8 program. All together, almost two-thirds (64%) of households in interest-subsidized Section 515 apartments were also benefiting from rental assistance.

Loans and grants can be made for low-rent housing for domestic farm labor, as authorized by Sections 514 and 516. Grants may cover up to two-thirds the costs of developing low-rent shelter for farm workers. However, activity under these programs has remained relatively small, perhaps because of reluctance of farm owners to assume responsibility. From 1950 to 1999, about 30,000 farm labor housing units have been provided with loans or combined loans and grants.

The Department of Housing and Urban Development has a recently established Rural Housing and Economic Development program. HUD's budget justification for FY2000 states that the department is working closely with USDA and other federal agencies to structure a more effective response to housing and high unemployment problems in rural areas. A major intended use is for technical assistance to enable rural areas to attract industry and to enlarge the capacity of nonprofit groups to promote economic development.

How the Programs are Administered

The USDA's rural housing loan programs are administered by 47 state offices and 807 local offices of USDA which provide direct services to applicants and borrowers. This extensive network can reach people in thinly populated areas, and partly explains why federal housing assistance in rural areas was largely shifted from HUD's predecessor agencies to USDA.[59] USDA's field staff have been delegated authority to make loans without waiting for approvals up the chain of command and thus can provide prompt service.

Who gets Housing Assistance?

Most of USDA's early housing assistance programs, with the exceptions of the farm labor and low-income repair loans, were targeted to moderate income borrowers who could not receive credit elsewhere on reasonable terms. Today, home loan borrowers who obtain interest-reduced loans from USDA have relatively low incomes. Average annual income of direct loan borrowers under the Section 502 program is about $17,000.

USDA's rental programs reach down to more deprived people. Almost nine in ten households in rental developments with interest-reduced loans (Section 515) have incomes below 50% of area median income. Annual income of Section 515 tenants in 1999 averaged $9,000. In determining the tenant's rent payment, income is adjusted for senior citizens, number of children, and other factors. After adjustments, income averaged $7,600.

Households headed by an elderly person comprised 41% of all households. Nonelderly families and individuals occupied 47% of the units;

---

[59] See Art Collings, "The Role of the Federal Rural Housing Programs," in Fannie Mae Roundtable, 1995, cited above.

nonelderly disabled or handicapped persons had 12%. White non-Hispanic families comprised 77% of tenants, blacks had 15%, and Hispanics and others had about 8%.

Domestic farm workers accommodated by USDA's housing programs typically have incomes below the national poverty threshold. Home repair loans (Section 504) are limited to very low-income people — incomes of 50% of area median or less — and home repair grants (Section 504) to older persons with very low incomes.

Problems in Rural Housing Programs

Over 80% of the elderly in rural areas are homeowners rather than renters. Some need help in maintaining and fixing their properties. USDA programs for homeowners, such as Section 502 loans and Section 504 grants, are not easily used by older households and many are reluctant or unable to take on long-term mortgage loan payments.

Reverse annuity mortgages, which enable older owners to convert home equity into monthly income while remaining in the property, are not very helpful to those with relatively low-valued properties, as would be the case with many low-income owners in rural areas.

Migrant farm workers have been described as the "working homeless." USDA can point to a number of success stories in housing and job training farm workers through assistance. If funds were available to replicate these successes in other places, USDA officials believe, a substantial dent could be made in the housing and social needs of such workers and their families.

Appropriations

In general, there has been a tendency to reduce spending year by year for rural housing programs and to move away from direct lending. Still, appropriations to construct new housing for low income families needing assistance, both owners and renters, have been continued, while similar construction programs of HUD have been shut down. USDA's homeownership loan programs (Section 502) are being tilted toward loan guarantees as against direct loans from the department. For FY2000, the appropriation for home loan guarantees is $3.2 billion, an increase of $200 million from FY1999. For subsidized direct home loans targeted to low- and very-low income families, the FY2000 appropriation is $1.1 billion, an increase of $134.7 million over FY1999.

Reductions in recent years in funding for additional multifamily developments under USDA's rental housing assistance program (Section 515) continue. For FY2000, $114.3 million has been appropriated, the same as for 1999, but lower than the $150 million provided in fiscal year 1998. The appropriation will make possible the construction of 1,742 new units and the rehabilitation of 1,487 existing units.

The rental assistance program (Section 521) will have $634.1 million in FY2000, an increase of $56.6 million over 1999, to supplement the rent of very low-income families.

Appropriations remain at modest levels for very-low-income (Section 504) homeowner repair loans and grants: $56 million for FY2000. For farm labor housing loans (Section 514) and farm labor housing grants (Section 516), the FY2000 appropriation includes $25 million and $13.9 million, respectively.

HUD's FY2000 appropriation includes $25 million for its Rural Housing and Economic Development program, the same as in 1999.

Chapter 6

COMMUNITY DEVELOPMENT BLOCK GRANTS AND OTHER PROGRAMS

THE COMMUNITY DEVELOPMENT BLOCK GRANT PROGRAM (CDBG)

Crime, noise, litter, and absence of adequate community facilities and services are leading complaints of residents in many city neighborhoods, older suburbs, and rural areas. Economic decline and job loss are the underlying reality in many places.

A HUD program that seeks to alleviate those problems is the Community Development Block grant, first authorized in 1974. It consolidated and replaced major categorical programs still remembered with some nostalgia by old urban hands including Urban Renewal, Open-Space Land grants, Sewer and Water grants, Neighborhood Faculties grants, and Model Cities, most of which dated back to the 1950s and 1960s. The advantages of a block grant, according to its proponents, are that states and entitlement communities do not have to apply for categorical funds each year and can do advance planning with the understanding that funds are likely to be available over a period of years. The allocation of funds by formula based on relative need gives some assurance of future funding, although money for the program is appropriated one year at a time.

How the Program Works

States, cities, urban counties and other units of general local government, along with other entities like Puerto Rico and recognized Native American tribes and Alaskan Native villages, are eligible to receive grants, and have wide discretion in the use of such funds. However, at least seventy percent of CDBG grants must be spent on activities that benefit low- and moderate-income persons over a period of up to three years. In practice, communities have used more than 90% of their CDBG allocation for such activities. There is no requirement for a local matching grant.

After certain set-asides, 70% of CDBG funds is allocated to entitlement communities and 30% to states for redistribution to small cities and counties. Entitlement communities are central cities and cities of 50,000 population or larger in metropolitan areas. Their allocations are based on one of two formulas that consider poverty, population growth lag, and age of housing stock. In 1998, 841 metropolitan cities and 145 urban counties were eligible to get grants by formula.[60]

To participate, entitlement grantees must submit to HUD a Consolidated Plan which identifies goals, programs, and projected uses of funds. Participating states must submit similar plans that explain their priorities and methods in distributing funds. Including places receiving funds through the states, more than 4,000 communities in urban, suburban, and rural areas received grants. Grantees are subject to an annual performance review by HUD. Performance indicators include the number of households assisted and jobs created as a direct consequence of CDBG and Section 108 funds, and local measures taken to actively advance fair housing practices. HUD has the authority, after an administrative hearing, to terminate or reduce funds according to review findings.[61]

Section 108 Loan Guarantee Program

This companion provision allows a participating jurisdiction to multiply its community development efforts by up to five times its annual CDBG grant. The grantee may pledge its current and future CDBG funds as the

---

[60] Data from HUD Budget Justification for 2000. Also, see CRS Report 96-503 GOV, *Community Development Block Grants: An Overview*, updated December 10, 1998, by Eugene Boyd.

[61] Data from HUD Budget Justification for 2000. Also, see CRS Report 96-503 GOV, *Community Development Block Grants: An Overview*, updated December 10, 1998, by Eugene Boyd.

main security for notes or other obligations issued to finance economic development, housing rehabilitation, or other activities. The borrowed funds may only be used for specific projects such as preserving industrial facilities or building inner-city shopping centers. Each project must be consistent with the Consolidated Plan and principally benefit low- and moderate-income people, or help to eliminate or prevent slums and blight, or address a particularly urgent community development need.

Activities

In entitlement communities, the largest single use of CDBG money is to rehabilitate neighborhoods and housing and to finance housing repairs. Economic development has become an increasingly important activity. In rural areas, the money is often directed to essential water and sewer facilities. In tribal areas, CDBG funds have been used to repair and weatherize houses, among other activities.[62]

Including places receiving funds through the states, more than 4,000 communities in urban, suburban, and rural areas received grants. Grantees are subject to an annual performance review by HUD. Performance indicators include the number of households assisted and jobs created as a direct consequence of CDBG and Section 108 funded activities, and local measures taken to actively advance fair housing practices. HUD has the authority, after an administrative hearing, to condition, reduce, or terminate funds in light of review findings.

Appropriation

CDBG annual funding levels have ranged between four and five billion dollars in recent years. The appropriation for fiscal year 2000 is $4.8 billion. Of this, substantial amounts are earmarked in the legislation for scores of specific activities and organizations in localities across the country, such as industrial parks, sewer and water facilities, and community centers.

Major set-asides include $240 million for grants for Economic Development Initiatives. These grants supplement loan guarantees under Section 108 which funnel private sector dollars into job creation and other community development activities. The FY2000 appropriation limits guaranteed loans to a total of $1.26 billion. The federal cost of guaranteeing

---

[62] *Ibid.*

such loans is shown as $29 million. This is a legislatively required budget "scoring" amount, but the federal government has never had to cover defaulted loans guaranteed under Section 108.

Separate funding of $25 million is provided for a CDBG-related activity called Brownfields Redevelopment, which promotes private development of new businesses and housing on formerly contaminated land physically cleaned up with money from the U.S. Environmental Protection Agency and federal tax credits.

Set-Asides Specific to Low-Income Housing

A substantial designation of $55 million within the CDBG total is for the *Resident Opportunity and Supportive Services program*. This provides funds for supportive services for public housing residents and grants for service coordinators as well as congregate housing services for elderly and disabled occupants of public and assisted housing.

An earmark of $20 million within the FY2000 CDBG promotes homeownership for low-income people through a *Self-Help Housing Opportunity program (SHOP)*. National organizations, regional nonprofit organizations and consortia with experience in using volunteer labor to build housing may apply on a competitive basis for self-help projects of at least 30 homes. Funds can be used to buy home sites and make infrastructure improvements not to exceed an average of $10,000 per home. Low-income purchasers must contribute a significant amount of work-time (sweat equity) to the construction. Grantees have included affiliates of Habitat for Humanity International and the Housing Assistance Council. Operating at a modest level-for the period 1996-1999 about 8,000 homes were planned — the program appears to fill a niche in the panoply of federal housing programs for low-income families.

SOCIAL SERVICES BLOCK GRANT PROGRAM (SSBG)

Administered by the Office of Community Services, Administration for Children and Families, in the Department of Health and Human Services (HHS), this program provides grants to states for certain services to vulnerable families and individuals to enable them to be self-sufficient and to maintain independent living. The federal funds are distributed to states by population and there is no requirement for matching funds.

How the Program Works

Within goals laid out in the authorizing legislation, states have wide discretion in the use of their allocation and in determining eligibility rules for participation by recipients. However, money transferred from TANF to SSBG must be used for recipients with incomes not in excess of 200% of poverty levels. Further, SSBG money may not be used for capital improvements, medical care, public education, or other specified purposes.

Who Benefits?

Information on how the funds have actually been used is hard to come by. A CRS analysis of FY1996 expenditures identified some major uses: child day care, foster care services for children, home-based services, and special services for persons with disabilities.[63] Students of housing will note that SSBG-funded social service activities help carry out goals of low-income housing programs of HUD and USDA. Housing and welfare experts now know that housing assistance must be effectively combined with social services if low-income families are to achieve self-sufficiency and family unification and the frail elderly and others unable to work are to live independently.

Appropriation

The appropriation for FY2000 is $1.775 billion, of which $425 million cannot be released to states until September 29, 2000. Funds for this program have been reduced in recent years from an annual level of $2.8 billion from 1989 to 1995. Its entitlement ceiling is set at $1.7 billion a year starting in FY2001. Reductions reflect views in appropriating committees of Congress that social services are funded by other federal programs, and that HHS lacks information on the effectiveness of activities supported by SSBG funds.

---

[63] For more information, see CRS Report 94-953 EPW, *Social Services Block Grant (Title XX of the Social Security Act)*, updated December 1, 1999, by Melinda Gish.

LOW-INCOME HOME ENERGY ASSISTANCE PROGRAM (LIHEAP)

The cost of energy for heating the house and using appliances is a heavy burden for many low-income families. Such costs, on average, took 9.3% of income of low-income households in 1995, compared with 2.5% for non-low-income households. The highest percentage burden is generally for low-income households using fuel oil, a common source of home energy in the Northeast and in older houses; those dependent upon kerosene or liquefied petroleum gas such as propane also have high burdens.

Congress addressed this problem in 1981 with adoption of the Low-Income Home Energy Assistance program (LIHEAP) and reauthorized it several times. It is intended to help people of very limited means with their energy bills for heating and cooling the house, heating water, and using appliances like stoves and refrigerators. In 1996, an estimated 4.3 million households received benefits for home heating or winter crisis relief, or both. The program has also provided emergency funds in states experiencing extreme heat waves, floods, or other natural disasters.[64]

How the Program Works

LIHEAP is administered by the U.S. Department of Health and Human Services (HHS) in coordination with the U.S. Department of Energy, which implements a weatherization program. Block grants are made to states, Indian tribes, and other jurisdictions. Grantees receive an allocation by formula based on heating costs, climate and other circumstances. There is no matching grant but states may supplement the assistance, and many do. California, Pennsylvania, and Ohio were among the largest contributors in a recent year. The actual sources were fuel funds, church and community groups, and utility rate assistance.

States and other grantees are expected to treat owners and renters equitably, to relate benefits to income and energy costs, and have a method for crisis intervention to deal with immediate needs. Within these requirements, states have considerable latitude in determining eligibility, types of benefits, and administrative arrangements, and are free of active federal scrutiny that federal guidelines are being adhered to.

---

[64] This program is more fully explained in CRS Report 94-211 EPW, *The Low-Income Home Energy Assistance Program: A Fact Sheet,* updated December 1, 1999, by Melinda Gish.

Who Benefits?

By federal statute, eligible households are those with incomes no higher than 150% of the poverty level or, if higher, up to 60% of state median income. About 4.3 million households got help with heating costs in 1996. For each recipient, there were three other eligible households who did not. Recipients spent an average of $1,089 for fuel, 11.3% of income. Average income of participating households was about $9,600 in 1995. Almost half of participating households had elderly or persons with disabilities.

Appropriation

The FY2000 appropriation for LIHEAP was $1.1 billion and another $300 million for emergencies, the same as for FY1999. Advance funding for FY2001 was set at $1.1 billion. Authorizing legislation sets annual program levels for FY2002-FY2004 at $2 billion.

THE NEIGHBORHOOD REINVESTMENT CORPORATION

This non-governmental organization was established by Congress in 1978 to revitalize declining neighborhoods and to help provide adequate housing within the means of current residents. It uses federally-appropriated funds to charter and advise local resident-led partnerships that include business men and women and local officials. These local groups, active in 181 communities in 1998, receive operating and equity grants which may be used to establish revolving loan funds and to make contributions to homeowners and to renters seeking to buy homes. The Corporation provides technical assistance to its chartered local entities. The local groups, in turn, offer a variety of help to residents, from pre-purchase counseling and down payment assistance to neighborhood clean-up and beautification activities. In the five years preceding 1998, the Corporation's network assisted with home-repair services to 40,000 housing units. Its staff estimates that each dollar spent by the Corporation has leveraged 11 dollars of investments by banks, savings and loan associations, insurance companies, and local governments.[65]

---

[65] Based on information from the research department of the Neighborhood Reinvestment Corporation received October 14, 1998. Some economists might note that some of the

Who Benefits

Households benefiting in 1997 from loans by the Corporation's local network were predominantly (70%) those with incomes below 80% of median income in their area. Median income of assisted purchasers of single-family homes (1993-97) was approximately $25,000. A substantial proportion of loans were made to African American families (36%), Hispanics and other minorities (24%), and the balance (40%) to non-Hispanic white families.

Appropriation

For fiscal year 2000 the Corporation has an appropriation of $75 million, a reduction of $15 million from the fiscal year 1999 funding level.

ROLE OF GOVERNMENT-SPONSORED ENTERPRISES: FANNIE MAE AND FREDDIE MAC

The Federal National Mortgage Association (Fannie Mae) and the Federal Home Loan Mortgage Corporation (Freddie Mac) are congressionally chartered corporations that serve as secondary market facilities in the purchase and sale of residential mortgage loans and the guarantee of securities backed by pools of mortgage loans. These government-sponsored enterprises (GSEs) are now the largest suppliers of residential mortgage credit in the country. Both are mandated to place a significant portion of their investments in housing for low- and moderate-income populations and in underserved areas.

In its previous life, the Federal National Mortgage Association was a federal agency within HUD and its predecessors. In 1968, it was partitioned into two entities, a private corporation, now referred to as Fannie Mae, to deal mainly with market-level mortgages, and an agency remaining within HUD known as Ginnie Mae to continue to support subsidized housing programs. Freddie Mac was established in 1970 at the urging of savings and loan associations which wanted "their own" secondary market facility. It

---

leveraged funds could have been forthcoming in the absence of assistance from the Corporation.

helps to maintain a national secondary market for conventional residential mortgages.

Fannie Mae and Freddie Mac are for-profit corporations, but their perception by the capital markets as government-affiliated enables them to borrow funds at a lower rate than strictly private companies. They make a profit on the spread between the yields on their investment portfolio and their cost of borrowing. They also make substantial fees in guaranteeing timely payment of principal and interest to investors in Fannie Mae or Freddie Mac mortgage-backed securities issued against pools of mortgages. These securities find a ready market among non-mortgage oriented institutions such as pension funds and insurance companies, thus joining real estate lending with the capital markets.

Fannie Mae and Freddie Mac are supervised by the Office of Federal Housing Enterprise Oversight for safety and soundness. They must meet goals to increase access to credit by lower-income borrowers and those in underserved areas. These goals are set by HUD.

Benefits to Home Loan Borrowers

The housing GSEs are a vehicle for subsidizing home borrowers and increasing the number of homeowners by passing on the interest savings they realize due to their government connection. They apparently do not pass through the entire saving to home borrowers; in a recent year they passed through about two-thirds of interest savings to borrowers and retained the balance, according to a study by the Congressional Budget Office.[66] Home borrowers save about one-third of a percentage point on GSE-involved loans. On a 30-year loan of $100,000 at 7%, this translates into a saving of about $20 a month.

Goals for Low-and Moderate-Income Borrowers

In the belief that the GSEs should make a larger contribution to social housing in light of the benefits conferred by their federal charters, Congress, in 1992, authorized HUD to establish annual goals for these companies in

---

[66] Congressional Budget Office, *Assessing the Public Costs and Benefits of Fannie Mae and Freddie Mac*, by Marvin Phaup, May 1996. CBO estimated that in 1995 the two corporations together saved $6.5 billion in interest costs due to government sponsorship and passed on $4.4 billion to home borrowers.

the purchase of mortgages on housing for low- and moderate-income families and underserved communities.[67]

The 1999 low- and moderate-income goal set for Freddie Mac and Fannie Mae on owner-occupied properties is to assist borrowers with incomes at or below 100% of area median income.

Their goal for underserved areas is to take mortgages on properties located in urban census tracts with median income at or below 90% of area median, urban and rural areas with a minority concentration of 30% or greater and median income at or below 120% of the area. Targeted rural areas are counties with a median income at or below 95% of the state or national nonmetropolitan median income.

Thus, the GSE goals can be satisfied with some loans to, or in behalf of, households with incomes higher than those eligible for participation in HUD- and USDA-assisted housing programs for "very low-income" and "extremely low-income" families (less than 50% and less than 30% of area median income, respectively).

How Much Risk are the GSEs Taking?

In financing home buying by low- and moderate-income families, the paramount question is who will take the risk of borrowers defaulting on their obligation to pay. With regard to home-purchase loans for lower-priced, FHA-eligible homes in metropolitan areas in 1994 (a rough proxy for lower-income borrowers), Fannie Mae and Freddie Mac together took 15 % of the risk. Banks and other depository institutions and FHA as a group accepted 56% of the risk. Similarly, the two GSEs together accounted for 10% of such loans made to black and Hispanic borrowers; FHA, banks and other depositories took the risk on 60% of such loans.[68]

Who are being Served?

Fannie Mae reports that it is making a special effort to serve low- and moderate-families, minorities, new immigrants, and families who live in central cities, rural areas and other distressed places. In 1994, the company

---

[67] Included in the Federal Housing Enterprises Financial Safety and Soundness Act of 1992. These goals can be viewed as the government imposing an in-kind fee on the GSEs.
[68] Based on findings by Glenn B. Canner and Wayne Passmore, "Credit Risk and the Provision of Mortgages to Lower-Income and Minority Homebuyers," *Bulletin,* Board of Governors of the Federal Reserve System, November 1995, pp. 989-1016.

made a trillion dollar commitment to serve 10 million households in targeted income levels and locations by the end of the year 2000. This commitment has been met, according to Fannie Mae. The company states that it exceeded its goals set by HUD for low- and moderate-income housing and underserved areas in 1997, 1998, and 1999.

Freddie Mac states that it more than met HUD's regulatory targets for low- and moderate income housing and underserved areas in 1998 and 1999. However, only a small proportion of single-family home loans were obtained by borrowers with very low incomes (less than 50% of area median). In multifamily rental apartments financed by Freddie Mac, a higher percentage of very low-income households could afford the dwellings.

Both Fannie Mae and Freddie Mac have invested substantially in low-income housing tax credits sold by developers of multifamily developments, but these are not counted toward GSE housing goals under HUD's rules.

In Sum

"There is room for further increases in purchases of affordable loans by Fannie Mae and, especially, Freddie Mac," according to studies by HUD's Office of Policy Development and Research.[69] In March 2000, the two companies were criticized by HUD's Federal Housing Commissioner for failing to make sufficient loans to black Americans.

In any event, these for-profit companies are not a vehicle for making deep and continuing housing subsidies for the poorest families, such as public housing and Section 8 rental assistance provide. They do participate in financing housing developments for lower-income renters and accept some of the credit risk on loans to marginal home buyers.

THE COMMUNITY REINVESTMENT ACT (CRA)

Banks and savings and loan associations are major suppliers of mortgage credit to home buyers. But in some areas, even where they may continue to accept deposits, they have tended to turn down applications for home loans on grounds that adverse neighborhood factors make such loans

---

[69] *The GSEs' Funding of Affordable Loans,* Working Paper No. HF-001, Office of Policy Development and Research, Department of Housing and Urban Development, by Harold L. Bunce and Randall M. Scheessele, December 1996. Other papers in this HUD series come to similar conclusions, as does the CBO study by Marvin Phaup, cited above.

too risky. The alleged practice, known as "redlining," automatically denied home loan applications in areas predominantly occupied by lower-income families, especially blacks and Hispanics.

The 95th Congress responded by adopting the Community Reinvestment Act (CRA) in 1977 (Public Law 95-128). Its purpose is to encourage banks and other depository institutions to help meet the credit needs of all sections of the communities in which they are chartered, including low- and moderate-income neighborhoods. This sometimes conflicts with the requirement that such lending be "consistent with the safe and sound operation of such institutions." The statute was amended in 1996 to reduce reporting requirements for banks with assets of less than $250 million, and further so in 1999.

Implementation

Federal financial supervisory agencies assess the performance of the banks and savings institutions in complying with CRA during regular examinations. These assessments are considered whenever an institution seeks approval of a new or relocated branch, merger with, or acquisition of, another institution or its assets, or similar changes. A bank or savings institution that has a rating of less than satisfactory for compliance with CRA may be denied its request. Community groups may contest an institution's application if they believe their area has been underserved. Few applications have been denied, but the performance ratings are a matter of public record and no doubt influence lenders to make credit available in low- and moderate-income areas. Credit that is covered includes not only home loans but small business loans, community development loans, and credit card lending.

Performance

Pledges of lending, investments, and services that meet the CRA criteria apparently have exceeded $1 trillion. How much of this activity would have occurred without the law cannot be ascertained, and the incomes or other characteristics of households or businesses actually benefiting are not known. In practice, loans made to comply with CRA may reach few families with poverty-level incomes.

Legislation

A number of provisions pertaining to CRA are included in the Gramm-Leach-Bliley Act (Public Law 106-102) signed into law November 12, 1999. A lending institution must be compliant with CRA to operate a financial subsidiary. The bank(s) of a financial holding company must be compliant if the company seeks to engage in new financial services activities. Banks with less than $250 million in assets are to be examined less frequently if they have a satisfactory or better rating unless they try to get a deposit facility. Interagency regulations to implement these provisions are scheduled for mid-2000.

Outlook

Modifications in the law in 1999 reflected calls by the industry to lighten the paperwork burden on depository institutions and to review actions by financial supervisory agencies to require CRA compliance for diversification into new activities. Industry people are likely to press for more regulatory relief along these lines. However, community groups strongly support CRA and insist on stronger enforcement by the financial supervisory agencies, and they have the support of the Clinton Administration.[70]

THE HOME MORTGAGE DISCLOSURE ACT OF 1975

This law directs banks and savings institutions which make federally-related housing loans to provide information on the number and dollar amount of loans made or purchased during the year. The information must be available to the public in a central repository of each metropolitan area and in the home office and a branch office in each metropolitan area in which the institution does business. The information must be provided by census tract, by FHA-, USDA-, and VA-insured or guaranteed programs and conventional loans, and grouped to reveal lending patterns by age of housing, income of households, and race and gender characteristics in the census tracts. The Federal Financial Institutions Examination Council has overall responsibility for this function.

---

[70] The CRA is the subject of CRS Report RS20197, Community Reinvestment Act: Regulation and Legislation, updated December 1, 1999, by William D. Jackson.

The information is analyzed for compliance with the CRA and fair housing laws. Studies by the staff of the Federal Reserve Board comparing outcomes for black and white applicants of similar incomes and other characteristics have concluded that blacks are less likely than whites to receive home loans. Some analysts, while not denying that discrimination occurs, have cautioned against simple interpretations of HMDA data, noting, for example, that some variables such as credit histories of applicants and differences in net wealth may not be taken into account.[71]

The banking industry views the assembling and provision of such information as a costly chore with little benefit. Some of the paperwork burden for very small banks was reduced by the regulatory relief provisions included in the omnibus appropriations act for 1997, (Public Law 104-208). Fair housing advocates insist that such information is vital in determining the degree of compliance with civil rights laws.

---

[71] See CRS Report 94-708 E, *Discrimination in Mortgage Lending: What Do We Know?*, September 1, 1994, by Barbara L. Miles.

Chapter 7

CONCLUSIONS

Since 1999 there has been a turnaround in federal support for low-income housing. After a hiatus of four years, funds have been appropriated so HUD could offer rental vouchers to new families to secure affordable housing. Operating subsidies for public housing were increased in the FY2000 appropriation along with modest increases for construction of housing for the elderly and persons with disabilities. And the rental housing assistance program of the U.S. Department of Agriculture has received a small increase in FY2000.

At the same time, a shift is occurring among beneficiaries of these programs. A growing view among officials and some lawmakers is that striving families, those who seek jobs or better-paying work, should be offered incentives. This is seen in the disregard of increases in income in the calculation of rent for a limited period for families who improve their situation, welfare reform, and recently enacted housing legislation that is intended to shift the mix of residents in public housing from extremely low-income to less poor families. But with limited funding, it is possible that assistance is being shifted from the most vulnerable populations like the impoverished elderly, the disabled, and others who cannot enter the labor force or who make no more than the minimum wage; that, in effect, income redistribution may be occurring within the low income population from the poorest to those with incomes closer to the median in the community.

A current theme is to enable as many lower-income renters as possible to become owners, despite absence of empirical support that homeownership by itself brings positive changes that benefit the rest of society. Much satisfaction is taken in the fact that the national rate of homeownership has risen to an all-time high, and getting the rate even higher is a Clinton

Administration goal. The downside is that some marginal families may be encouraged to purchase but ultimately lose their property and credit rating if incomes drop as a result of unemployment, illness, or other misfortune. In previous efforts along these lines, federal insurance funds have been lost and some families left by the wayside. Reportedly, FHA is now beginning to show some caution in insuring loans for low-income families where sellers finance down payments, then mark up the home price to cover down payments.[72]

A sense that federal agencies are too inflexible and remote from local circumstances has given rise to the growth of block grants with broad discretion vested in state and local governments and well-managed public housing authorities. The federal agency role is being reduced to allocating funds by formula and to after-the-fact monitoring (increasingly by private contractors) of spending by fund recipients. One consequence is that relatively little is known about the results of such grants except general information about types of activities getting money. In the past, this was the case with community development block grants, one of the most popular programs among mayors and other local officials because of the autonomy they enjoyed. The law requires that most of the money be spent in low- and moderate-income neighborhoods, but this still allows money to be spread among many wards by local officials. Steps are now being taken to obtain more detailed information from participating jurisdictions on the use of such funds. The HOME block grant is reportedly well targeted to constructing or fixing housing for low-income families, with discernible results that fulfill the goal.

An associated approach in this search for "a third way" is to empower neighborhood associations to decide on changes to their neighborhoods. This is not new: under the old urban renewal program citizen participation was one of the prerequisites to securing federal money. What is different is the set-asides of HOME funds for nonprofit community-based housing development organizations and the increasing professionalism of those who run or advise these neighborhood associations under the HOME program.

There are many anecdotes of success, but it is difficult to evaluate actual performance of the newer approaches and overall results in relation to needs. Some nonprofit development organizations participate in the low-income tax credit program in partnership with corporate investors like Fannie Mae and also receive block grant funds. The piecing together of several subsidies is

---

[72] The Washington Post, October 27, 1999, p. E3.

necessary to develop housing affordable by very low-income families when the low-income tax credit is the main vehicle.

The only housing programs *standing alone* which can reach the poorest families are HUD's public housing and Section 8 rent assistance vouchers. But they are expensive and, unlike tax credits, stand out in the budget, so they had been curtailed in the process of reducing federal budget deficits. Now, with a budget surplus, the Congress and the Clinton Administration appear to be more willing to increase funding for low-income people in need of housing help. The Administration's budget for FY2001 proposes a doubling of incremental Section 8 vouchers from the FY2000 level of 60,000 to 120,000 units, but requests relatively small increases for the public housing capital fund and operating fund.

Budgetary considerations aside, some housing analysts believe that both new low-income housing construction and vouchers for use in existing housing are necessary. The mix will vary from area to area depending upon the tightness in the rental housing supply and the availability of accommodations for special populations such as the elderly, persons with disabilities, and the homeless. Available data indicate that the gap between rent-paying ability by low-income Americans and the supply of affordable housing has widened in recent years.[73]

Economic growth has raised the income and living standards of many Americans. But not all. The number of low-income families in need of housing help actually increased in the past decade, while the supply of affordable unsubsidized rental housing declined. Economic growth alone does not lift all boats when it comes to housing the poor. If housing opportunities are to be extended to the disadvantaged and to newcomers, more effort will be needed-by the federal government, the communities, and the poor families themselves.

---

[73] *Rental Housing Assistance – The Worsening Crisis,* U.S. Department of Housing and Urban Development, March 2000, cited above.

INDEX

A

acquired immunodeficiency syndrome (AIDS), 48-51
advocacy groups, 22
appropriations, 1, 2, 33, 40, 41, 49, 57, 72
Asia, 8
Asians, 26
assisted housing, 1, 9, 11, 13, 15, 40, 43, 50, 62, 68

B

backdoor financing, 24
Bankhead-Jones Farm Tenant Act, 54
Below Market Interest Rate (BMIR), 11, 23, 24, 27
black households, 7
blacks, 26, 57, 70, 72
block grant funds, 11, 74
block grants, 31, 34, 53, 74
building deterioration, 5
Bureau of Indian Affairs, 53
Bureau of the Budget (BOB), 24
Bush Administration, 42
business, 15, 38, 48, 53, 65, 70, 71

C

child support, 14, 38
children, 3, 4, 6, 7, 15, 16, 26, 28, 38, 49, 51, 53, 54, 56, 63
cities, 1, 3, 5-8, 13, 16, 23, 34, 54, 60, 68
Clinton Administration, 33, 42, 71, 74, 75
Community Development Block Grant Program (CDBG), 34, 53, 59-62
Community Housing Development Organizations (CHDOs), 34
community improvement, 12
Community Reinvestment Act (CRA), 69, 70, 71, 72
concentrated poverty, 6
construction programs, 57
Continuum of Care program, 50
credit needs, 70
crime, 6, 18, 49
crime prevention, 19
crops, 8
crowding, 5, 6

D

Department of Agriculture, 9, 11

depository institutions, 68, 70, 71
development costs, 24
direct loans, 46, 54, 55, 57
disabled, vii, 11, 26, 29, 38, 46, 48, 57, 62, 73
displaced families, 20, 21, 23
domestic farm workers, 8
drug abuse, 6
drug activity, 18, 19

E

economic development initiatives, 61
elderly, vii, 11, 15, 16, 18, 26-29, 38, 45-49, 54, 56, 57, 62, 63, 65, 73, 75
endless lease, 40
enhanced vouchers, 9, 31
entry-level jobs, 10
entry-level wages, 8
Environmental Protection Agency, 62
extremely low-income, 4, 9, 31, 68, 73

F

fair market rent (FMR), 35, 38, 40
family income, 17
Fannie Mae, 43, 54, 56, 66-69, 74
Farm Security Administration, 14
Farmers Home Administration, 54
Federal Home Loan Mortgage Corporation (Freddie Mac), 66-69
Federal Housing Administration, 23
federal housing assistance, vii, 4, 56
Federal National Mortgage Association (Fannie Mae), 24, 66
federal occupancy preferences, 21
federal programs, 1, 11, 63
financial solvency, 17
fixed incomes, 25, 29

G

General Accounting Office (GAO), 15, 20, 32, 33
general assistance, 10, 14, 38
ghettos, 7
government spending, 26
government-sponsored enterprises (GSEs), 66-69
Gramm-Leach-Bliley Act, 71

H

Health and Human Services (HHS), 9, 10, 62-64
Hispanic renters, 6, 8
Hispanics, 26, 57, 66, 70
home buyers, 69
HOME funds, 11, 34-36
HOME Investment Partnerships Program (HOME), 1, 11, 12, 31, 34-36, 74
home loans, 55, 57, 69, 70, 72
Home Mortgage Disclosure Act (HMDA), 71, 72
Home Ownership and Opportunity for People Everywhere, 42
homeless, vii, 3, 7, 10, 21, 47-50, 57, 75
homelessness, 3, 6, 47-49, 51, 52
homeowners, 1, 3, 11, 34, 35, 41, 43, 57, 65, 67
Homeownership and Opportunity for People Everywhere (HOPE), 20, 41-43
HOPE 1, 42
HOPE 2, 42
HOPE 3, 42, 43
HOPE VI, 21
Housing Act of 1961, 23
Housing and Community Development Act of 1992, 51
Housing and Urban Development (HUD), 1-6, 8-11, 14-16, 18-21,

25, 27-31, 34-42, 46-48, 50-61, 63, 66-69, 73, 75
Housing and Urban Development Act of 1968, 41
housing assistance, 9, 10, 39, 50-52, 56, 63
housing counseling services, 36
Housing Opportunities for Persons with AIDS (HOPWA), 50-52
housing problems, vii, 1, 3, 8, 11, 46
housing programs, 12, 18, 27, 43, 57, 62, 63, 66, 75
housing supply, 3, 9, 39, 75

I

income distribution, 3
income problem, 5
income-based rent, 21
Internal Revenue Service (IRS), 11, 30, 31

J

job training, 50, 57
joblessness, 6

L

Latin American countries, 8
loan management set aside, 24
local housing authorities, 1
Los Angeles, 1, 13
low income families, 17, 57
Low Income Housing Tax Credit (LIHTC), 31-33
low-income families, vii, 1, 2, 5, 11, 34, 36, 40, 42, 43, 55, 58, 62-64, 74, 75
Low-Income Home Energy Assistance Program (LIHEAP), 64, 65
low-income households, vii, 36, 43, 64, 69

Low-Income Housing Tax Credit(s), 1, 11
low-income renters, 8, 41, 43
low-rent housing, 14, 55

M

management of public housing, 19
management performance, 19, 30
market-priced housing, 13
mark-to-market, 29, 30
matching funds, 34, 62
media, 42, 54
median income, 4, 17, 21, 22, 26, 28, 32, 35, 51, 55, 56, 65, 66, 68
mental health, 47, 48
mental illness, 49
metropolitan areas, 4, 22, 39, 54, 60, 68
Mexico, 1, 8
middle class, 3
minority households, 39
mixed-income developments, 1, 23
modernization, 14, 18, 19, 23
mortgage credit, 54, 66, 69
mortgage loans, 52, 66
mortgages, 23, 24, 29, 30, 55, 57, 66-68

N

National Affordable Housing Act, 34, 42, 46, 48, 51
National Housing Act, 25
Native Americans, 8, 26, 52, 53
Neighborhood Reinvestment Corporation, 65
neighborhoods, 2, 6, 13, 16, 23, 39, 59, 61, 65, 70, 74
New Approach Anti-Drug program, 19
new construction, 23, 27, 31, 36, 41, 53
Newark, 1, 13

Nixon Administration, 27
nonprofit entities, 1, 24

O

occupied dwellings, 4, 5, 8
Office of Federal Housing Enterprise Oversight, 67
older persons, 28, 57
operating costs, 18, 24, 29

P

Pacific Islanders, 26
Participating Administrative Entities (PAEs), 30
pensions, 14, 24, 38
Performance Funding System formula, 18
permanent housing, 47-50
Personal Responsibility and Work Opportunity Reconciliation Act, 9
persons with disabilities, 15, 27, 46, 47, 63, 65, 73, 75
physical defects, 4, 5, 8
population change, 8
poverty line, 39, 52, 54
poverty threshold, 4, 38, 57
poverty-level families, 1
privately-owned dwellings, 8
project-based subsidies, vii, 29, 39
property taxes, 14
public housing, vii, 1, 2, 10, 13-25, 28, 37, 40-42, 46, 48, 49, 53, 62, 69, 73-75
public housing agency (PHA), 10, 14, 17-22, 37, 38, 40
Public Housing Assessment System, 20
Public Housing Capital Fund, 18
public housing communities, 2
public housing development, 18
Public Housing Drug Elimination Program, 19

Public Works Administration, 14

Q

Quality Housing and Work Responsibility Act of 1998, 1, 21, 40

R

redlining, 70
rehabilitation, 5, 9, 11, 13, 24, 27, 30, 31, 34, 36, 38, 40-42, 48, 53, 58, 61
rehabilitation of housing, 12
rent, vii, 1, 3, 4, 8-11, 14, 15, 17, 21, 24-31, 35-40, 45-47, 49, 52, 54-56, 58, 73, 75
rent certificates and vouchers, vii, 39
rent receipts, 10, 14, 17, 18, 25
rent reduction, 33
rental assistance, 1, 10, 11, 24, 32, 34-36, 46-48, 51, 55, 58, 69
rental housing, vii, 8, 23, 29, 35, 37, 45, 55, 58, 73, 75
rental housing markets, 8
rent-paying ability, 10, 47, 75
repair, 5, 18, 54-58, 61, 65
Resident Opportunity and Supportive Services program, 62
rural housing, 55, 56, 57
Rural Housing Service (RHS), 31, 54

S

Safe Havens, 48
Section 8, 1, 2, 9-11, 20, 22, 24, 27-31, 37, 38, 40, 41, 45, 48, 55, 69, 75
Section 8 New Construction and Substantial Rehabilitation program, 27
Section 8 rent certificates/vouchers, 1, 37

segregation, 7
Self-Help Housing Opportunity program (SHOP), 62
set-asides, 60, 61, 74
shelter(s), 3, 5, 7, 9, 10, 27, 47, 48, 50, 54, 55
shelter cost, 5
Shelter Plus Care program, 48
single-parent families, 17
Single-room occupancies (SROs), 48
Social Security, 10, 14, 24, 28, 38, 63
Social Services Block Grant Program (SSBG), 62, 63
state housing finance agencies, 1
Stewart B. McKinney Homeless Assistance Act, 47
subsidies, 1, 10, 11, 14, 17, 22, 24, 25-27, 29, 31, 33, 37, 39, 45, 53, 55, 69, 73, 74
suburbs, 5, 6, 7, 54, 59
Supplemental Security Income, 10, 14, 28, 38

T

targeted dwellings, 21
tax credits, 31, 33, 34, 62, 69, 75
tax-exempt bonds, 31
teenage pregnancy, 6
Temporary Assistance for Needy Families (TANF), 9, 10, 14, 38, 63

tenant-based assistance, vii, 11, 32, 38
tenant-based vouchers, 2

U

U.S. Department of Agriculture (USDA), 1, 11, 15, 42, 52, 54-58, 63, 73, 68, 71
unassisted renters, 4
unemployment, 14, 38, 52, 56, 74
unemployment benefits, 14, 38
United States Housing Act of 1937, 14
utilities, 4, 18, 28, 45, 52, 54

V

vouchers, 2, 20, 22, 30, 37-41, 43, 73, 75

W

wages, 15, 24, 26, 38, 39, 53
welfare assistance, 9
welfare families, 9, 10
welfare programs, 1
welfare reform, 9, 73
welfare to work, 1, 2, 10, 41
working families, 2, 20, 53